Marijuana

Harvest

MARIJUANA HARVEST

Maximizing Quality and Yield in Your Cannabis Garden

Copyright © 2017 Ed Rosenthal
Published by Quick American Publishing
A division of Quick Trading Co.
Piedmont, CA

Printed in North America
Second printing

ISBN: 978-1-936807-25-3
eISBN: 978-1936807-26-0

Cover Photo: Ed Rosenthal
Project Director: Jane Klein
Project Manager: Angela Bacca, Rolph Blythe
Editors: Angela Bacca, Rolph Blythe, Susan Lang
Editorial Assitance: Araxi Polony, Darcy Thompson
Cover Design / Art Direction: Christian Petke, D-Core
Interior Design: Pauline Neuwirth, Neuwirth & Associates
Library of Congress Control Number: 2017937965

All photos by Ed Rosenthal unless otherwise noted.

Marijuana

Harvest

Maximizing Quality and Yield

in Your Cannabis Garden

Ed Rosenthal
and David Downs

QUICK AMERICAN PUBLISHING

Acknowledgments

A special thanks to Alan and Alix at C.R.A.F.T., Americover, Angela Bacca, Barry from Ultra Trimmer, George Bianchini, Rolph Blythe, Sidney Borghino, Boulder Cannbis, Tom Bruggerman and Amy Beal from Tom's Tumble Trimmer, CaliKind Farms, Scott Cathcart, James Cox, Steve DeAngelo, Stephen Dillon, Andy Domico, Jay Evans, Ganja Ma Garden, Reggie Gaudino Ph.D, Green Man Cannabis, Green Pad, Mark Gray, Groco Rentals, Ryan Hall, Ivan Handelsman, Harborside Health Center, Joshua Hoffman, Ellen Holland, Kevin Jodrey, Alise Jusic, Kenny and Ben from Trim Bag, Jane Klein, Dave Lampach, Nikki Lastreto and Swami Chaitanya, Brian Lundeen, John Mackay, Robert Martin, Method Seven, Tod Mikuriya, Jeremy Moberg, Dana Mosman, My Pharm Jar, Jonathan Nielson, Alex Nikas, North Bay Cultivators, North Coast Cultivators, Northern Emerald Farms, North Star Genetics, Jerry Norton, Casey O'Neill, Christian Petke, Rick Pfrommer, Araxi Polony, Cullen Raichart, Rambling Rose Farms, Charles "Charly" Rutherford, Jason Schulz, Steph Sherer, Skunk Bag, SPARC, Felicia Sparkman, Steep Hill Labs, Gart Swanson, Darcy Thompson, True Humboldt Farms, Josh Trinity, Jonathan Valdman, Chris van Hook, Adam Weiss and Spencer Uniss, Mark Wortham, Josh Wurzer, Scott Yandell, George Zimmer and all my friends on Facebook and Twitter.

Dedication

This book is dedicated to the pioneers of legalization—Mike and Michelle Aldrich, Dana Beal, Steve DeAngelo, Ben Dronkers, Tom Forcade, Debby Goldsberry, Jack Herer, Ben Masel, and Dennis Peron. The world would not be the same without you.

"Speeding arrow, sharp and narrow/
What a lot of fleeting matters you have spurned/
Several seasons with their treasons/
Wrap the babe in scarlet colors, call it your own/
Did he doubt or did he try? Answers aplenty in the bye and bye/
Talk about your plenty, talk about your ills/
One man gathers what another man spills."

"St. Stephen" —Written by Jerry Garcia, Phil Lesh and Robert Hunter

Contents

Introduction   viii

1   Why Harvesting Is So Important   1
2   Harvesting Basics   5
3   Harvesting Strategies   17
4   Finishing   39
5   Flushing   49
6   Ripening   63
7   Picking   81
8   Trimming   109
9   Drying   145
10   Curing   167
11   Storing   185
12   After the Harvest   195

Sponsors   214
Sources/Bibliography   241

Introduction

IF YOU'RE PICKING UP this book you probably know—we're living in exciting times.

In North America, and elsewhere in the world, cannabis is asserting or reasserting itself like never before. One in five Americans now lives in a legalized state. Entire countries are adopting similar measures. The medical legitimacy of cannabis has emerged out of its modern Dark Age. For the first time in history, pharmaceutical companies in Europe, and hemp oil factories in Kentucky are growing strains that are numbered, not named.

We are at the dawn of cannabis as a modern crop science. Articles are being published in agronomy and chemistry journals and soon, we'll see entire journals devoted to cannabis., and eventually, libraries of it at places like University of California Davis.

What follows in this book is the third draft of that science. It follows Ed's *Marijuana Grower's Guide* and the *Marijuana Grower's Handbook.* Cannabis cultivation—and harvesting in particular—is evolving from a folk art to an agricultural field. Hundreds of papers are waiting to be written about topics like optimal terpene preservation and chemical changes associated with flushing.

In writing this book, we studied prior research, conducted controlled experiments, communicated with researchers and went all over the country interviewing cultivators and working to systematize that knowledge.

They let us into their nurseries, their veg rooms, their bloom rooms. We asked questions: What mistakes did they make along the way? Where do they want to take their craft? What's holding them back?

And we combined that field reporting with what Ed does best: fearlessly question and innovate. What's impressed me the most about working with Ed is his daringness to hypothesize, and his egolessness when it comes to discarding disproven ideas. It's the difference between the expert, and the genius—that drive to relentlessly question and propose a new way of doing things. The fortitude to potentially be wrong, and indeed, see progress in failure. . . . It strikes me that Ed was 'failing fast' decades before it was a Silicon Valley mantra.

This type of relentless innovation is important. With legalization comes the erasure of cannabis' once-fat profit margins, and the rise of intense competition, on price, cleanliness, quality and uniqueness. Commercial growers are going to have to never stop optimizing and that dynamic will only benefit consumers. As for the one's growing it themselves–they'll find it more rewarding, with cheaper, cleaner, better-tasting homegrown for themselves and their loved ones.

Please enjoy, *Marijuana Harvest*. And don't hesitate to get in touch. After all—the thing about science is advancing knowledge.

—David Downs, May, 2017

1

Why Is Harvesting So Important?

HARVESTING, DRYING, CURING AND and storing are incredibly important processes to growers. Each contributes to the final quality of the flowers. A good crop followed by a poor harvest is as disastrous as crop failure. It's post-crop failure.

The goal of this book is to preserve and even improve the quality of your crop by showing you how to pick, cure and prepare your flowers and leaves for a variety of uses.

THE EVOLUTION OF HARVESTING

Growers usually plan their gardens in great detail by setting timetables and cultivation parameters for their plants and bringing the plants to the peak of maturity. However, they often spend a lot less time planning the harvest.

Even large commercial operations are sometimes far behind in harvest and post-harvest operations. These final tasks need the most thought; they are the ones most likely to be improperly executed—but they needn't be. With proper preparation the process can flow seamlessly.

Whether you are a sole practitioner or putting together a harvest team, try to divide up the tasks so there are few bottlenecks. The task flow can be divided in many ways. For instance, if a grower has access to an area to store branches or colas but insufficient trimming facilities, they ought to prioritize bringing in the buds and pulling off fan leaves. The colas can be placed in storage to dry before trimming or under refrigeration to keep them fresh for wet trimming. Then the material can be manicured over a longer period of time.

No matter what the situation, plan ahead and prepare for the coming harvest.

Hand manicured fresh buds cultivated by C.R.A.F.T. Cannabis
[Photo by Gracie Malley]

The harvest consists of several tasks:

- Cutting the colas from the plants
- Cutting the buds from the branches
- Trimming the buds
- Drying the buds
- Curing the buds

Make sure to prepare for each stage. In many cases, even on large farms, not much has changed over the years. Growers tend to get set in their ways; their gardens are easily dated by the techniques they employ. Not all growers realize new equipment is available to increase efficiency and cut down on the manual labor associated with the harvest.

If buds aren't processed correctly, a perfectly good crop can be destroyed. Proper harvesting includes keeping the buds clean and fresh and preserving flavors and aromas.

Marijuana's freshness is based on two factors: maintaining enough moisture in the material for it to be pliable without inviting mold and, just as important, retaining the terpenes found in the trichomes. The terpenes are volatile oils that evaporate at different temperatures, some of them as low as 68° F (20° C). For this reason, at no time during the drying and curing process should the temperature be raised very much above this point.

Before it is consumed, marijuana is judged first by appearance and then by smell. Fresh, aromatic buds are the most likely to be demanded and consumed. This book will show you the best methods and latest technologies not only to properly harvest your marijuana garden, but also to finish the job right.

It's imperative to plan ahead, know the bottlenecks and schedule accordingly but, most importantly, as a grower, it is important to know what you are doing and why.

Enjoy the harvest.

Commercial drying space [Photo by Rick Horn]

Kierton T4 Tumbler type industrial grade trimmer

Kosher Kush by Nadim Sabella

2

Harvesting Basics

Harvesting takes place at the end of flowering when the buds are at their peak ripeness, before the plant's psychotropic or medicinal resin begins to degrade. It consists of multiple processes done in a specific order: cutting down plants, their colas or buds, removing their leaves, then drying, curing and storing for later use or for processing into buds, extracts, edibles and other products.

Even a small harvest requires a little bit of labor. Processing a large one adds complexity and requires planning. Determining when to cut the crop, whether to cut whole plants or to judge each bud for its ripeness, when to trim, how and where to dry and cure the buds for use or processing, how to preserve the aroma and taste by retaining the terpenes and essential oils, are important decisions for any harvest.

If the plant is small, it is more likely that all the buds will ripen at the same time. On larger plants, the outermost exposed parts of the buds, the first 3-6 inches (7.5-15 cm), may ripen before the inner buds. Another consideration is that different varieties have unique ripening patterns. Buds ripen from the top down on some varieties, and all at once on other varieties. Consider that in a garden of mixed varieties the ripening times may vary by several weeks. These factors may also affect growers' harvest strategies.

Small gardens with a yield of ten pounds (4.5 kg) or less allow for more flexibility during harvest time. Growers with larger yields, especially those that ripen over a short period of time, require more elaborate preparations. Indoors, where plants are harvested on a weekly or monthly basis, harvesting becomes a routine task.

CANNABIS LIFE CYCLE

Cannabis is a fast-growing annual plant that does best in well-drained, high-nutrient growth mediums and long periods of bright, unobstructed light.

The plant starts out as a small oval brown seed and usually grows vegetatively for several months before starting reproductive growth or flowering. It begins flowering when it receives at least nine to eleven hours of uninterrupted darkness, depending on the variety, each 24-hour period. Outdoors in the northern hemisphere, depending on variety and latitude, flowering usually begins between late July and September and ripening between September and November. Using light deprivation, some outdoor growers manipulate the light cycle to harvest in the summer. Indoor growers control flowering by adjusting the light regimen. Flowers reach peak potency in seven to ten weeks.

WHEN ARE THE BUDS READY TO HARVEST?

Begin planning for harvest when the flowers ripen, between six and eight weeks after the beginning of flowering.

No bud should be picked before its time. Plants and varieties differ in maturation pattern. Some mature all at once, so that the whole plant can be picked. Other varieties mature from the top down, or alternately, from the outside in. For these varieties, the buds on the outside mature faster than inner buds hidden from the light. Once the outer buds are harvested, the inner branches are exposed to light and quickly ripen. It can take two weeks of choosing mature buds before the plant is totally picked. Picking the plant a little at a time ensures that every bud is at maximum potency and quality.

A plant's flowering cycle, and its ripening and harvesting-time, are variety specific. Each variety is programmed to respond to a critical period of darkness that turns growth from vegetative to flowering. Indoors, this is accomplished when the lights are cut back to twelve hours. Outdoors, the critical time period varies between about nine and eleven hours of darkness.

In addition to genetics, flowering time is also affected by light intensity and total light received on a daily basis, ambient temperature and nutrients.

The best way to determine the picking time is by watching the development of the trichomes (the stalk-like resin glands that contain the active compounds), which grow on the leaves surrounding the flowers.

HPS lamps produce an amber light that makes it difficult to examine plants in the garden. Method Seven lenses filter the light and correct it for better vision.

The flower area becomes covered with resin glands over time. The length of this stage of growth usually lasts two to three weeks; in modern varieties these glands ripen in seven to nine weeks from flower initiation. Late-season and long-maturing varieties usually spend about three to five weeks in this period of heavy trichome growth.

As flowers near ripeness, their caps swell with resin and the trichomes become more prominent and stand erect. The viscous, sticky liquid that accumulates contains terpenes and cannabinoids, which are produced on the inside membrane of the trichome cap. As the resin accumulates in the cap, the flower odor becomes more intense.

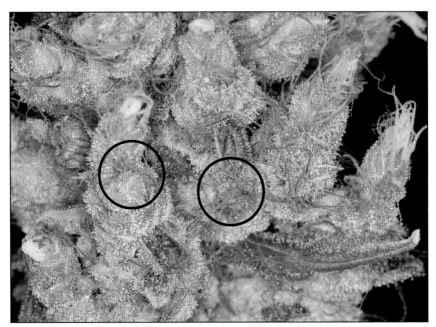

A swollen calyx is one indication of ripeness. Here are two examples. This is a false seedpod; the flower has not been fertilized and no seeds develop.

Stalked capitate trichome with bulbeous trochome circled [Photo by Professor P.]

Types of Trichomes

▶ **Bulbous Trichome**

    Bulbous trichomes have no stalk and are much smaller than the other trichomes. They appear mostly on leaves rather than in the bud area, especially during vegetative growth, and contain cannabinoids.

▶ **Crysolith Trichome**

    These trichomes do not contain cannabinoids. They grow on the bottom of the leaves to deter pests.

▶ **Sessile Stalked Capitate Trichome**

    These trichomes appear during the vegetative growth stage and produce only small amounts of cannabinoids.

▶ **Stalked Capitate Glandular Trichomes**

    These trichomes are the most abundant and contain the desired cannabinoids, terpenoids and flavonoids that growers seek.

The Kind Scope offers 60X. It is easy to watch development and choose the time to pick under 60x magnification lit by UV and LED lights. It is lightweight and portable and comes in bright colors to help prevent misplacement.

The odor reaches its peak at the same time the trichomes begin to fluoresce in the light, twinkling like little crystals. In some varieties, the trichomes are so prominent that the whole bud sparkles. Using a magnifying glass, a photographer's loupe or a microscope, monitor the buds' progression to the peak of ripeness by watching the resin in the gland tops. Under magnification, you can see individual glands turning from clear to amber or a cloudy white. These colors indicate that THC is beginning to degrade into two other cannabinoids, cannabicyclol (CBL) and cannabinol (CBN), which are not nearly as psychotropic as THC. **When the trichomes begin to change from clear to amber or cloudy white, the buds should be harvested—this is the peak moment.**

Ripe cannabis reeks of pungent terpenes and each day brings increased intensity of odor. Rub the leaves surrounding the bud between clean fingers and inhale. This releases aroma molecules while leaving fingers sticky with resin. Inhale and smell an exotic medley of familiar and unusual odors that may range from sweet to acrid with outlying musks and skunks.

Ripening Facts

▶ **Plants of the same variety flower and ripen at about the same time. Clones from a single plant grown under the same conditions flower and ripen at the same time.**

▶ **Flowering time is determined by the light regimen, not a plant's age or size.**

▶ **When all the buds on small plants get direct sun, they tend to ripen at the same time.**

▶ **Buds on large plants that are directly lit, whether on the top of the plant or the sides, mostly ripen at the same time.**

▶ **Outdoors, big plants grown with large spaces between them will often get light from three different sides as the sun moves around them, specifically from the east, west and south. This light pattern is especially prevalent in the fall when the sun is at an acute angle and lower on the horizon.**

▶ **On large colas, outer buds often ripen while the inner buds are deprived of direct sunlight.**

Closely manicured buds cultivated by C.R.A.F.T. Cannabis
[Photo by Gracie Malley]

HARVESTING EARLY OR LATE

Many growers determine when to pick based on the 30/70 rule. They harvest when approximately 30% of the trichomes have turned amber and the remaining 70% are milky white. By this time much of the THC has degraded to CBN and has lost potency. For the most potent buds possible, harvest as soon as the first trichomes turn amber or white. If the purpose of the buds is to treat insomnia, CBN is the desired cannabinoid and the plants should be picked later than usual, when they are over-ripe.

Some growers assume they can harvest early to produce plants with higher CBD levels. This is not true. Harvesting early, under-ripe buds, only produces an end product with less overall cannabinoid content. Cannabis will not continue to ripen after it has been harvested.

The Evolution of Cannabinoids and Terpenes

Cannabis evolved cannabinoids and terpenes not for human enjoyment but for protection. That's why they become so concentrated during the flowering cycle. As the plant flowers and nears fruiting, it invests more energy in growing and protecting its seeds.

Cannabinoids and terpenes protect the plant in many ways, including:

▶ Repelling and trapping insects
▶ Deterring birds and mammals from eating by disorienting them
▶ Acting as antibiotics and fungicides
▶ Protecting the plant from ultraviolet (UV) light

Because THC protects the plant from UV light, adding a UVB light to an indoor garden encourages the plants to produce more THC. Using light deprivation outdoors, enables growers to harvest in the summer, when UV light is at its annual peak.

END PRODUCTS

Growers often segment the harvest into different end-product categories. The finest buds are harvested, processed and sold as top-shelf flowers, while less visually appealing buds and trim are harvested and processed for use in extracts and edibles.

Left: Concentrate Mr Nice B. Supermelt.[Photo by Nadim Sabella]
Right: Concentrate The Pure Sativa Supermelt. [Photo by Nadim Sabella]
Bottom: Edibles packaging is evolving from craft based to commercial.
[Photo by JustinCannabis@7stars]

*It's important to keep buds upright so they don't encroach on neighbors'
canopy space. Here, monkey ties hook onto branches, then pull them upright.*

Garden Profile: North Coast Cultivators
Santa Rosa, Sonoma County, California

MARKET: Medical
SIZE: 52 lights
LIGHTING: Indoor HPS
MEDIUM: Soil
YIELD: 3 pounds (1.4 kg) per crop, approximately 169 crops annually

North Coast Cultivators provides both dispensaries and patients with a regular supply of a wide variety of strains, including Blackberry Kush, Mango, Durban Poison, God's Gift, Sour Diesel, Gorilla Glue and their exclusive variety J27. To meet the regular demand, a series of cabinets is set with plants at various stages of growth, allowing North Bay to harvest high-quality buds perpetually.

Left: *The soft cloth containers are placed in trays on 2/4's with casters for easy Mobility. A wet-dry vacuum quickly sucks excess water from the trays.*

Right: *Vegetative plants are trained using tomato cages that keep them from spreading out.*

The plants' nutrient needs are met through a proprietary blend of liquid nutrients. The plants grow to 4-5 feet (1.2-1.5 m) tall. They are set to a harvesting schedule the moment they are planted. Each plant is inspected for pests daily. Toward the end of flowering, trichomes are monitored daily to determine the perfect day to cut.

Each bud is harvested individually as it ripens. A large machete is used to slice branches with ripe buds away from the main stem. The branches are then de-leafed and hung to dry. Five full-time trimmers are employed to trim the buds once the plants are dry.

North Coast Cultivators says its biggest challenge is maintaining the perpetual harvest while also staying ahead of changing laws and keeping the entire operation legally compliant.

Harvesting Strategies

BEFORE LAYING OUT A strategy, determine your garden's goals. If the crop is to be used for its flowers, then the harvesting method will be different than that utilized for extracts and concentrates. As with any blooms, cannabis flowers should be handled gently and with care. Plants used for extracts or concentrates can be handled without concern for cosmetic beauty.

There are many strategies to consider. Some require planning during variety selection or before planting while others can be decided later in the season. Numerous factors play a part in these decisions.

FACTORS TO CONSIDER

One of the first major decisions a grower faces is how big the growing area will be. Whether planning for hobby growing or a large commercial operation, the goals should be realistic. Assess the resources required in labor and capital and determine whether those resources are available to meet the expenses of production.

With that in mind, consider labor as a factor of time. The main labor factors are setup and harvest. Both of these operations can be carried out over a longer period of time by a smaller group, or in a shorter time by a larger group.

Personnel and Timing

A smaller group can more easily handle a crop that is harvested over several weeks versus a crop that is harvested all at once.

Hand-cutting ripe buds in a greenhouse. [Photo by David Downs @SPARC]

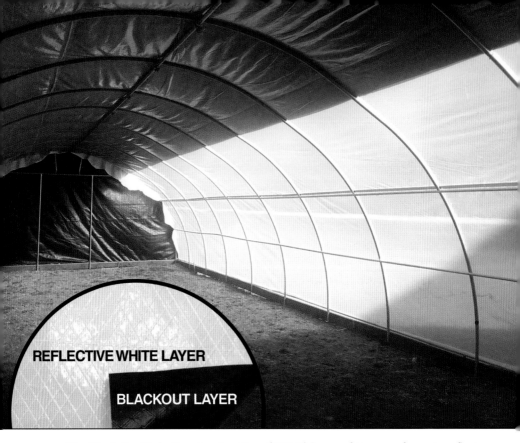

REFLECTIVE WHITE LAYER

BLACKOUT LAYER

The Black Out Light Deprivation Tarp (BOLD) has a white outer layer to reflect sunlight, keep the space cool. The black inner layer ensures complete light deprivation. It is light and heat resistant, and certifiably organic. BOLD Tarps are made from tough, reinforced, and tear resistant material.

Varietal Differences in Ripening Time

Each variety has an expected ripening time. When a single variety is grown, all the plants will have ripe buds at the same time. When several varieties are grown, a different variety could ripen every few days over the span of a month or longer.

Large sativas and sativa hybrids often have buds 1 foot (30 cm) or longer. Sometimes the outer 6 inches (15 cm) are ripe, but the inner portion hasn't yet ripened because it was partially shaded by the branch above. Cut the ripe portion and leave the unripe. Once the inner portion is exposed to more direct sunlight, it will ripen in a week or less.

Whether the growing space is planted with large plants of a single variety or several varieties with different maturation times, harvesting only mature

Right: Light deprivation is used to induce plants to flower and ripen earlier in the season, offering intense summer light for flowering and often averting bad weather.

buds and leaving the rest will improve the quality of the crops and extend the harvesting period. Doing so will require fewer workers who are employed over a longer period of time.

Light Deprivation

Outdoor growers can induce plants to flower early using light deprivation. Using this technique plants are placed under the sun but receive only twelve or thirteen hours of light daily and eleven or twelve hours of uninterrupted darkness using shade curtains. This causes the plants to flower, no matter their size or age. With the use of light deprivation, ripening can be times for early harvesting, to avoid fall weather, or to produce multiple harvests.".

There are various ways to utilize light deprivation outdoors without building a greenhouse. Growers using containers on rollers can move their plants around with the sun and bring them indoors when it is time for darkness.

Others use hoops draped with white-black panda plastic to create darkness. The white color on the outside reflects light and prevents heat buildup, keeping the plants cool. The black on the inside prevents light from reaching the plants, extending the dark period necessary to induce flowering.

These Forever Flowering Northern Latitude greenhouses use automated light supplementation and deprivation to control flowering and harvest times. They resist snow and wind loads and have active and passive climate controls creating a cozy environment for plants all year-round.

Light or darkness is available on demand. Growers create a controlled environment using the sun's natural energy, saving electricity and reducing strain on the environment.

Greenhouses are used all year long to harvest several crops, to start plants for transplanting or to test new varieties. Greenhouses can be constructed for many of environments, resisting southern heat and northern cold. They make gardening easy because many of the operations can be automated. Supplemental lighting and passive climate control allow farmers to maximize production any time of year.

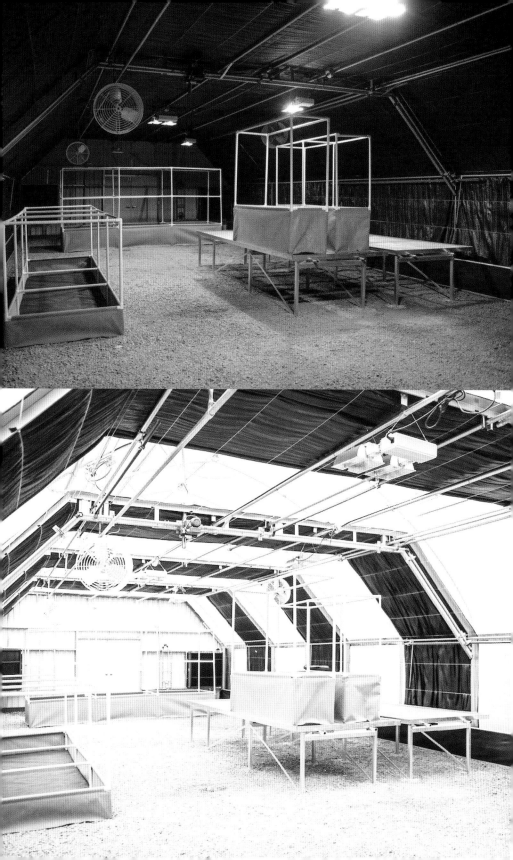

Weather

Marijuana is a fall-flowering plant. At the time when plants could use more light energy, energy of sunlight is naturally declining, beginning in early to late August through Autumn. At the same time the weather may change from balmy summer to cool fall, sometimes with wind and rain—weather not always conducive to great buds.

A grower may have to make hard decisions and compromises. Consider the following situation: the buds are ten days from early ripeness. The weather forecast is for cool weather followed by rain and then a long period of sun and warm weather, long enough to ripen the crop. What to do? Cut early and forfeit ripeness or leave the plants standing and take measures to try to prevent mold attacks? (See *Picking* for more information on this topic.)

SUPPORT

Long and heavy branches should be supported both indoors and out.

Indoors, framed netting with 6-inch (15 cm) holes allows the buds to grow through and then supports them so they don't lean over. Stakes and monkey ties are another easy method of supporting plants and branches. Sometimes supporting the main stem is all that is required. In other situations, individual branches may need extra support.

Outdoors, supports are usually not needed for small plants, especially if they are being grown as a "sea of green" because plants within the group hold each other up.

Supporting large plants can play a crucial role in a successful harvest for several reasons:

- Without support, limbs heavy with buds sometimes break.
- During rain or windstorms an unsupported plant can be damaged or even uprooted.
- Supported buds won't infringe on other buds' space.

6" square fencing was used to enclose this young plant. The fencing will support the center stem as the plant grows. Branches are already growing through the squares as the plant spreads out.

WORKING WITHIN PLANT AND CANOPY LIMITS

Restrictive laws that limit cultivation are usually based either on canopy area or plant count. Space or canopy-restricted fields produce most efficiently when they are filled with a multitude of plants. Each plant must grow only a small amount before it is forced to flower; this way a plant may spend only two to three months in the ground before harvest and the space can be used for three, four or more crops per year.

Left: Netting is stretched across the canopy to hold the buds in place and to support the laden branches. [Photo by David Downs @ Bolder Cannabis.]

Bottom Left: Small plants decrease turn-around time because the vegetative growth period is short. [Photo by David Downs @SPARC]

Bottom Middle: Bamboo stakes are used to keep the central stem upright and to support the side stems. [@Green Man Cannabis]

Bottom Right: Example of a single small plant [@Green Man Cannabis]

Plants in this sea of green garden were spaced a foot apart.

Indoors, a sea of green canopy absorbs virtually all light, leaving little in the shadows below. For this reason, the understory below the canopy contributes little energy to the plant. Instead, it costs the plant nutrients, increases humidity and stops airflow.

Restrictive plant count regulations promote the growth of monster plants that yield fifteen pounds (about 7 kg) of flowers or more. A plot of large plants must be configured with enough space between the plants to prevent them from shading each other. This is of most concern in the Fall when the sun hangs lower on the horizon; so space the plants far enough apart so they don't shade one another.

What to Harvest

Large plants: A large plant, whether tree-like or bushy, that has basked in the sun all season may be covered with colas from top to bottom. Every area kissed by the sun has branches with leaves and buds to capture the light. Remember, however, that the buds only occupy the perimeter of the plant. The interior is made up of bare stem and a framework of bare branches supporting the vegetation.

The harvester has a few choices: cut the whole plant or big sections of it; cut individual branches; just the ripe buds and leave the rest to ripen; or cut all the buds, separating them into A's for ripe and B's for premature.

Let's look more closely at these options. Why would a grower consider cutting the whole plant? Perhaps weather conditions are severe enough to require a rapid harvest; or, if the grower is working with a crop that ripens evenly and is ready to harvest at the same time, s/he may choose to cut whole plants in order to harvest the entire crop at once. The choice may revolve around labor availability. A grower can choose a large crew to cut and dry the product all at once, a surge crew to work for a limited period of time, or, depending on financial constraints, a crew to trim when demand for labor is lower.

A single large plant can produce 15 lbs. of bud. The perimeter fence helps keeps the plant upright.

Another choice is to cut individual branches as they mature. Cutting off the outer branches opens the inner buds to light, hastening maturity and providing more light to the undeveloped sections.

A grower may trim individual buds for the same reason—doing so provides the immature buds more light. But other factors may lend themselves to harvesting only the buds. If the weather is predicted to stay fair for a long period, a grower may choose to change the flow of his/her harvest by slowing the process down and trimming off the best buds as they become perfectly mature.

You may choose to sort buds or branches into A's and B's, using the material for different purposes. If you are feeding a machine, cutting individual branches is often preferable. Before using the trimming machine, perfect buds are separated from lesser quality buds. The shake and imperfect buds are used for concentrates while high quality buds are trimmed.

Small plants: With smaller plants, often most of the buds are ready at the same time. Either the whole plant can be cut at the stem or the colas can be cut.

All material that is removed from the plant should be placed on tarps, in bags or in plastic bins for transfer to the processing space.

PRUNING

Pruning increases yield of some varieties. Indoors, removing lower limbs creates more airflow, lowers humidity and stops the lower leaves' use of sugars produced in the upper leaves, maximizing yield.

Super-cropping can improve yield by training top branches to grow horizontally, quickly filling the capony and providing consistent light throughout.

PRUNING TECHNIQUES

Pruned plants occupy more space than plants left unpruned, so yield per plant increases substantially with pruning. Pruning techniques must be adjusted to each variety's growth habit.

Employing the proper pruning technique will result in low stress training.

Plants can be pruned to become bushy rather than tall, trimmed to only a few branches, cut to fit a space, or stretched out to promote branching. Pruning off smaller branches early in flowering increases bud production of the remaining branches.

To make a plant bushy, clip the tip of the growing shoot after the third set of leaves has developed. This releases branches surrounding the top branch, which has inhibited growth, and creates a rosette of three or four large branches. Other lower branches will grow a bit as well. To make the plant even bushier, clip the top again after the plant has grown another three or four sets of leaves. Sometimes the plant is pinched once or twice more during the vegetative stage. Cutting the tip encourages a plant to spread out rather than grow vertically.

If plants are spaced apart so they receive light on their sides as well as their tops, then the side branches that look promising should be left on the plant. Prune off small or weak branches with small buds that slow large bud growth.

A lollipop plant. Lower branches are removed to prevent foliage from getting near the ground and picking up pests and dirt.

Flat Plants

Selective pruning can be used to create flat two-dimensional plants that can be placed against walls, positioned close to each other or placed in unusual configurations.

Cannabis typically grows leaves on opposite sides of the stem, with each set of leaves perpendicular to the next. Each leaf is attached to the stem at approximately a 90° angle, parallel to the ground, positioned to catch light. Opposing branches develop at the nodes between the leaf and stem, so the plant has four corners.

With the removal of branches from every other set of leaves, plants have branches that are opposite each other in two dimensions. This technique can be modified to remove only one branch from every other set of leaves, so one set of branches juts out at a 90° angle from the opposing pairs, creating a more triangular shape. This way, the flat side can be placed against a wall, while the others project into the space.

Floribunding (Fimming):

Trim the top 80% of the apical growing tip, leaving about 20% intact. The tip develops multiple tops creating a bushy plant laden with heavy branches. Topped branches usually develop two to four new tops for each cut. When this technique is used, a single branch produces six to eight tops.

Fan Leaf Removal for Light

Contrary to popular belief, most fan leaves should not be removed from the plant during the vegetative stage. These leaves are costly for the plant to produce; they are sugar factories that turn light into chemical energy. The sugars are used for powering metabolism and for building tissue by combining with nitrogen and phosphorous to make amino acids and proteins. When a leaf that is catching light is removed, the plant loses a source of energy, slowing its rate of growth. When fan leaves are routinely removed from plants, growth slows and yields diminish.

Sometimes a few fan leaves block light from a large section of the plant. Remove these leaves if it results in a better distribution of light.

Remove leaves that block light from getting to buds or the cola. Dark spots become more apparent as the buds grow and become more prominent. Retain leaves that are not blocking light from the buds.

Single-Bud Plants

Plants can be put into the flowering cycle when they are only 8 in - 2 feet (30-60 cm) tall, before they have developed branches. They grow into plants with only one bud. The main stem becomes swollen with flowers, but there is little to no branching. These plants are useful for compact gardens because each requires only 1 square feet (232-930 sq cm) of floor space.

FLUSHING

Over fertilized, unflushed buds leave a harsh chemical taste on the roof of the mouth and upper throat. Another sign of over fertilized, unflushed buds is the color of the bud's ash. A flushed bud produces white ash while a nutrient-laden bud produces black ash. Flush or leach outdoor plants for 10 to 15 days. Don't water for one to two days before harvesting—the water is only going to have to be dried out later. (For more, see *Finishing & Flushing.*)

MOLD

Buds infected with powdery mildew or other molds and fungi are unfit for smoking. Many jurisdictions mandate laboratory testing of commercial cannabis for fungal and bacterial pathogens.

Moldy buds are not suitable for use in extracts either. Concentrating contaminated cannabis using ice water transfers toxins and spores into the final extract, making it unfit for smoking. Moist hash molds when stored at room temperature.

Butane and carbon dioxide extractions kill mold and mildew but leave toxins behind. As a result, professional extractors in legal states are facing mandatory lab testing.

PREVENTING MOLD

Botrytis (gray or brown mold) is found almost everywhere and infects many plants, including marijuana. The fungus, which germinates only on wet plant tissue when the temperature is between 55-70° F (13-21° C), consumes the plant. It can attack both live and drying buds.

Mold grows when buds are grown or dried in an environment that is too humid or when incompletely dried buds are sealed in air tight containers. Once mold starts growing, it tolerates a wider range of humidity and temperatures. After mold depletes the oxygen in a sealed container, anaerobic bacteria become active, turning the buds brown and crumbly. A sure sign of anaerobic bacterial activity is an acrid ammonia odor.

When buds are dried and cured properly, they rarely become infected with mold. The best way to deal with infection is prevention.

Wet marijuana is 80% water. Molds colonize plant matter which contains as little as 15% water, so it's important to dry quickly, and in as controlled a fashion as possible without sacrificing terpenes. This is done by keeping humidity under 50% and not raising the temperature above the low 70's. With low humidity, the air is not saturated and absorbs moisture faster.

Mold and fungal spores are mobile; they are in the air and on surfaces. They require a temperature of 60-75° F (15.5-24° C), high humidity and an acidic environment to germinate. When humidity is kept below 50% and the leaf surface alkaline, mold spores are prevented from germinating. When the cannabis plant is alive, it has natural defenses that fight off constant attacks by pathogens. As soon as the plant is harvested, it is subject to attack by botrytis, aspergillus and penicillium.

Aspergillus is a common mold that thrives in oxygen-rich plant environments. It causes sinus and lung infections in people with compromised immune systems and has been implicated in some of the few recorded deaths related to marijuana. Smoking marijuana is safe, but inhaling mold spores isn't.

Previous Page: Brown mold [Photo by Kim Kemp]

Top: Powdery Mildew

Bottom: Aspergillus

MICROBIAL CONTAMINANTS IN CANNABIS:
What are the Dangers?

By Reginald Gaudino
V.P. of Science Genetics and Intellectual Property
at Steep Hill Labs, Inc.

Molds, bacteria, and yeast are present everywhere, including in the air we breathe. Unless cannabis is grown in a clean room with appropriate air filtration and other good growing and laboratory practices, it is inevitable that these microorganisms will be found on cannabis flowers and products made with them. Most microorganisms do not present a problem at low levels, though some pathogenic microorganisms are harmful even at low levels because they produce toxins that cause a variety of symptoms: from allergy-like symptoms to various types of cancer. Other microorganisms are harmful at mid to higher levels of contamination, particularly if they are inhaled. Immunocompromised patients, including those receiving chemotherapy, are at a higher level of risk to all microorganisms, where even low levels of microbial contamination can lead to fatality. Contaminated medical cannabis and incidence of diseases such as Aspergillus nodulosis (a disease caused by the inhalation of Aspergillus niger) has already been noted.[1]

Recently, Steep Hill Labs collaborated with medical researchers at University of California, Davis - Medical Center, and found that of 20 randomly selected samples submitted for testing at the Steep Hill Facility in Berkeley, California all had detectable levels of microbial contamination, and many had significant pathogenic microorganism contamination.[2] The variety of potentially harmful bacteria and fungi found was surprising and included: Klebsiella, Pseudomonads (several, including P. aeroginosa), Enterobacteria (including both pathogenic and non-pathogenic forms of E. coli), Acinetobacter (several, including baumannii), Aspergillus (including niger), Fusarium, Mucor, Penicillium, Botryotini, and many other

1 Fatal aspergillosis associated with smoking contaminated marijuana, in a marrow transplant recipient: R Hamadeh, et al. Chest. 1988;94(2):432-433. doi:10.1378/chest.94.2.432, Salmonellosis Associated with Marijuana—A Multistate Outbreak Traced by Plasmid Fingerprinting D.N. Taylor, M.D., et al. N Engl J Med 1982; 306:1249-1253, Aspergillus: An Inhalable Contaminant of Marihuana N Engl J Med 1981; 304:483-484

2 Thompson et al, "A Microbiome Assessment of Medical Marijuana", Clinical Microbiology and Infection (2017), doi: 10.1016/j.cmi.2016.12.001

bacteria and fungi. Some of the samples studied harbored multiple potentially pathogenic microorganisms (e.g., Aspergillus, Fusarium, Penicillium, Enterobacter, Pseudomonas).

Because the presence of microbial contaminants often results in the byproducts of growth being left behind, sterilization of the product does not necessarily ensure the product is completely safe for consumption. Sterilization of the contaminated substance may kill live microbes, but it does not remove the presence of the microbes (DNA, proteins, and/or lipids left behind), or remove the toxins certain microbes leave behind. The DNA, lipids and proteins from microbial contaminants, whether pathogenic or nonpathogenic, also have the potential of acting as antigenic determinants on their own, and could lead to a full range of allergy-like reactions. If the cannabis contaminated with pesticides, mycotoxins or endotoxins is destined for extraction and concentration, there is a significant risk that the contaminants, particularly pesticides, will be concentrated and pose greater risk to the end user.

Pharmaceutical grade medical Cannabis can be produced using Good Growing Practices (GGP). This requires clean grow rooms/green houses, complete humidity and ventilation control, HEPA filtered air systems and gowned workers wearing hair covering; essentially the same practices used to produce pharmaceutical products. Without this infrastructure, it is impossible to avoid microbial contamination, which leads to pesticide usage.

Pesticides add another level of risk to the Cannabis end user. Thresholds targeted in those states that do require pesticide testing are based on information from studies done on skin contact or ingestion. None of the research conducted studied pesticide inhalation. So the levels being considered aren't relevant to potential harm or risk mediation for the intended use. It is likely that many of the pesticides used will have very different effects, and at much lower levels, due to their introduction through the lungs while smoking.

It has already been well publicized that Myclobutanil, the primary ingredient used to control fungal infestations (particularly powdery mildew), turns to Cyanide gas. Further investigation into the effect of all pesticides used on Cannabis is needed, as are experiments to identify the types, if any, of microbial contaminants that pass through the smoke stream. Investment in these Standard Operating Procedures will enable the production of more consistent Cannabis products between batches, assuming identical or nearly identical genetics are used each growing cycle.

To ensure the safety of any Cannabis flower product, but particularly medical Cannabis, DNA based microbial testing methods (e.g., PathogenDx, qPCR, DNA microbiome sequencing) must provide the necessary scientific rigor to ensure compliance with pharmaceutical standards.

Detection of DNA indicates that a particular species was resident on the plant at some point; absence indicates the complete lack of colonization of the flower by whichever species. Detection of a species known to produce toxins should require testing for that toxin. Absence of the toxin, and presence of the microbe below levels established for specific patient groups, would allow certification of the product for use by some patients and adult users. If toxin residue or pesticides or serious microbial contamination is detected, the product could be evaluated for remediation (e.g., chemical extraction and fractionation to produce extracts free of the contaminant).

OVER-RIPE FLOWERS

Over-ripe flowers can be identified in several ways. First, the trichomes turn color as the resin they contain degrades from THC to CBN. Sometimes new white stigmas grow from the buds. Over-ripe buds grow "bananas," single male flowers that take the shape of the yellow fruit. They form late in the growing cycle so any pollen they produce will not affect the flowers. However, cosmetically they are disastrous; they drastically reduce a bud's value.

Over-ripe flowers do have a use. They produce all-female pollen, meaning any seeds will be female. They produce all-female pollen, meaning any seed produced will be female.

Some high-CBD/THC strains reach peak CBD levels earlier than THC levels. Letting them ripen fully leads to increased THC levels.

Overripe bud with "bananas". These are male flowers that appear as the unpicked flower teeters past maturity. Seed created using pollen from these flowers produce all female plants.

4

Finishing

UNDERSTANDING ESSENTIAL PLANT ANATOMY

Budding stage cannabis plants require large amounts of nutrients. Using an enriched soil or nutrient solution dissolved in water ensures that the plant is getting enough nutrients. In order to understand the finishing process, it helps to know how the plant absorbs nutrients.

The roots of the cannabis plant are connected to the two vascular (think circulatory) systems: the xylem and the phloem.

The xylem carries water from the roots to the branches and leaves. A combination of surface tension and adhesive forces, formally known as capillary action, allows the plant to pull the water up the stem against gravity.

The phloem is the part of the system that carries sugars, hormones, enzymes and wastes from the upper canopy down to the lower portions of the canopy, the stem and ultimately the roots. The roots flush and exude sugars, enzymes and wastes that are digested by micro-organisms in the rhizosphere, the area surrounding the roots that supports micro-organisms including mycorrhizae. There is no indication that the phloem carries raw nutrients, the dissolved solids that make up fertilizers, out of plants.

Since cannabis is such a valuable crop it is sensible that farmers try many methods and techniques for enhancing crop quality and yield. Fertilizer companies have introduced dozens of products for bud enhancement, many of which are described below. The companies have followed two paths, nature and science.

Ripe Bud [Photo by David Downs @Ganja Ma Garden]

Well-known growth and flower enhancers such as humic acid, kelp, molasses and sugars, guano, and mycorrhizae increase crop performance by enhancing the root environment, which increases ability to absorb water and nutrients that stimulate the plant's growth.

Formulas dependent on the new botanical sciences include: amino acids, vitamins SAR stimulators, as well as plant hormones to increase quality and yield while shortening ripening time.

FINISHING PRODUCTS

All finishing companies keep their formulas proprietary. However, they all work based on one of two theories. They either bind the nutrients so they are no longer available to the roots (whether they remain or are washed away), or they make the salts more soluble so they flush out of the soil easily.

Earth Juice Sugar Peak is a molasses-based nutrient designed for maximizing production. Begin using 14 days prior to harvest. Both Earth Juice product can be used in soil and hydroponic gardens.

The following chart lists a range of finishing products readily available in stores and online. This chart and the appendix that follows list the specific ingredients comprising various finishing formulas.

CHART OF FINISHING PRODUCTS

PRODUCT NAME	COMPANY	INGREDIENTS
Bud Burst	Nutrifield	Dried kelp
Buddha Bloom	Aurora Innovations	Bat Guano, Worm Castings Soy Protein, Kelp Extract Molasses, Yucca Extract
Amino Aide	Aurora Innovations	Kelp, Yucca, Amino Acids L-Arginine, L-Arginine, L-Glycine
Big Swell	Aurora Innovations	Yucca, Molasses, L-Glycine, Phosphoric Acid, Potassium Hydroxide
Bloombastic	Atami	P2o5,K2o , Chelated Fe
Bio Bloom	Biobizz	Molasses, Seaweed
Ripe	Botanicare	Cano3, Mgso4, Kno3, Kh2po4, Po4, Mnso4, Ammonium Molybdate
Liquid Karma	Botanicare	Dolomite, K2co3, Co3, Fish Meal, Seaweed Extract, Mgso4, Humic Acid, B Vitamins
Sweet Grape	Botanicare	Mgso4, Feso4 (Probably Contains Synthetic Flavor And Odor Enhancers), Ers, Sugar
Sweet	Botanicare	Same As Above
Bountee Better Bloom	Bountea	Fish Protein, Kelp, Vegetable And Mineral Extracts
Bloom	Cutting Edge Solutions	MgSO4, KSO4, KH2PO4, POLYPARABAN (On the consumer watch lists of dangerous chemicals), Potassium sorbate. (There may be other unidentified chemicals as well because the last two ingredients listed are preservatives, which are not needed for the other listed ingredients.)
Sugaree	Cutting Edge Solutions	K2SO4
T-Rex	Cutting Edge Solutions	B1, Glutamine, L-Cysteine (Supplementation causes increased growth and more branching.)
Oily-cann	Earth Juice	MgSO4, CaCO3, humic acid
Hi-Brix	Earth Juice	KO2, Molasses
Sugar Peak	Earth Juice	Earth Juice, Molasses, Phosphates, KHSO4
Zyme	Cyco	Amylase (an enzyme that catalyzes the hydrolysis of starch into sugars.)

PRODUCT NAME Finishing Products	COMPANY	INGREDIENTS
FlavorFul	Humboldt Nutrients	Refined humic acids
Sugar Peak Grand Finale	Earth Juice	Kelp, bat guano, fossilized guano,, Molasses
Europonic Nitrozyme	Hydrodynamics International	Algae extract
Flowering Organic Growth Stimulator	Sierra Natural Science	N, P2O5, K2O, Kelp. Extracts of radish and wild carrot (Queen Anne's Lace), Molasses, humic acid
Bud Factor X	Advanced Nutrients	Chitosan, Surfactant
Big Bud	Advanced Nutrients	L-tryptophan, L-Cysteine, L-Glutamate and L-Glycine, P, K
Nirvana	Advanced Nutrients	Humus, seaweed extract, (Laminaria saccharina) and alfalfa meal, yeast, quilla and yucca extracts, hydrolyzed whey protein, ein, bat guano, azomite
Overdrive	Advanced Nutrients	MgHPO4, MgSO4, KH2PO4, Citric acid, mixed amino acids
Terpinator	Rhizoflora Inc.	K2SO4

Soul Synthetics Amino-Aide is a complex amino acid blend specifically formulated to increase vigor and yields. It can be used in both or soil and hydroponic gardening.

Soul Synthetics Big Swell is formulated from botanical extracts, amino acids and versatile carbohydrates combined with a specific ratio of readily available phosphorus and potassium. Soul Big Swell can be used as an additive in conjunction with any base nutrient program designed to increase yield.

Salmon River OG [Photo by Professor P @ Dynasty Genetics]

GLOSSARY OF COMMON FINISHING INGREDIENTS

ALGAE EXTRACT Kelp extract

AMINO ACIDS Primarily glutamine and cysteine, but includes others. May be absorbed through the root system, increasing stress tolerance, growth, yield and vitality.

AMMONIUM MOLYBDATE Molybdinum (Mb) micro-nutrient

AMYLASE An enzyme that acts as a catalyst for breaking down starches, turning them into sugars. These sugars provide a source of energy for the plant

ASCORBIC ACID Vitamin C

AZOMITE A natural mineral complex that stimulates growth.

B VITAMINS Use of B Vitamins noted in literature or practice.

B1 VITAMIN Touted as a stress relief for plants. Proven to have no value.

B2 VITAMIN Also known as Riboflavin. There is no direct literature or note of its use in plants, which produce it in abundant quantities. However, it is known to protect some organisms from UV light

BAT GUANO Source of organic N or P

BONE MEAL (STEAMED)
(N:1.6-2.5, P:21, K:0.2) Moderate release source of P

CACO3 Calcium carbonate, source of Ca

CARBOHYDRATES Simple sugars such as glucose or dextrose that plants can uptake

CARROT (WILD, AKA QUEEN ANNE'S LACE) Ferments into amino acids that stimulate flower growth

CHARCOAL Soil conditioner that stimulates plant growth.

CHELATED	Many micro-nutrients are metals that have little availability. When bonded with other elements (chelation) they become much more available.
CHITOSAN	Found in crustacean shells, insect exoskeletons and fungus cell walls. Plant growth enhancer, and bio-pesticide substance that boosts the innate ability of plants to defend themselves against infections .
CITRIC ACID	Vitamin C. When sprayed under stress conditions, improves growth and internal citric acid concentration, and also induces defense mechanisms by increasing the activities of antioxidant enzymes. May play a positive role in stress tolerance.
CYSTEINE (L)	An amino acid high in sulfur. Effective against bacterial infections in plants and may stimulate terpene production.
DOLOMITE	Mined combination of Ca (lime) and Mg
EXTRACT	A preparation containing the active ingredient of a substance in concentrated form
FE	Iron
FESO4	Iron sulfate
FISH MEAL	Made from ground fish byproducts and non-food fish, 60-70% protein. A rich source of amino acids
FISH PROTEIN	Concentrated fish meal
GLUTAMINE (L)	(Glutamate) An amino acid involved in plant growth. Supplementation may increase stress resistance and growth
GUANO	Seabird or bat poop
HUMIC ACID	A complex of acids that result from the decomposition of plant matter. It contains humic and fulvic acids as well as other molecules. It helps to regulate the bio-availability of nutrients to the roots.

JASMONIC ACID	Regulates plant growth and development processes including growth inhibition, senescence, flower development and leaf abscission.
K2CO3	Potassium carbonate, a common fertilizer
KELP	The seaweed, ascophyllum nodosum.
KH2PO4	Potassium phosphate, a common fertilizer
KHSO4	Potassium hydrogen sulfate (potassium-bisulfate); a common fertilizer
K2O	Potash, a common fertilizer
KH2PO4	Potassium phosphate, a common fertilizer
KNO3	Potassium nitrate, a common fertilizer
K2SO4	Potassium sulfate, a common fertilizer
K	Potassium, always used as a compound
MICRONUTRIENTS (MICROS)	Elements used by plants in small quantities. They are: boron (B), zinc (Zn), manganese (Mn), iron (Fe), copper (Cu), molybdenum (Mo) and chlorine (Cl). In total, they constitute less than 1% of the dry weight of most plants.
MYCORRHIZAE	Fungi that grow in association with plant roots in a symbiotic relationship. Ectomycorrhizae form a cell-to-cell relationship with the root hairs. Arbuscular mycorrhizae penetrate the root cells. Both provide nutrients and protection in return for root exudate containing their food, sugars.
MG	Magnesium, an essential element
MGHPO4	Magnesium phosphate
MGSO4	Magnesium sulfate aka Epsom Salts
MNSO4	`Manganese sulfate- Micro-nutrient

MOLASSES	Sugar concentrate made from sugarcane
N	Nitrogen
*NIPACIDE	Biocide. Kills all living organisms. Made from formaldehyde. DO NOT USE.
P	Phosphorous, Always used as a compound
*PARABEN	Widely used in cosmetics as a preservative and bactericide and fungicide. Weak association as an estrogen simulator and with endocrine interruption. DO NOT USE.
PHOSPHATES	Phosphorous compounds
PO4	Phosphate
P2O5	Phosphorous pentoxide, commonly used fertilizer
*POTASSIUM SORBATE	Preservative and fungicide commonly used in foods and cosmetics
PHYTO-ACIDS	(Bloom Master, Earth Juice). Undetermined plant products.
RADISH	Ferments into amino acids which are growth stimulators
SAPONINS	Derived from Yucca. Reduce water surface tension and loosens minerals from around roots
SEAWEED	Kelp
SUGAR	Plant food supplement that can be absorbed by roots
TRIACONTINOL	Plant growth stimulator. Large quantities are found in alfalfa.
TRYPTOPHAN (L)	Boosts flower hormone production

*DO NOT USE

5

Flushing

FLUSHING AT FLOWER INITIATION

To get the full effect of the change of cycle, rapidly flushing the old nutrients out and replacing them with the new flowering formula, rather than vegetative growth formula, hastens flower initiation. Some brands suggest at least a partial flush periodically during flowering.

Flushing may be the most controversial subject covered in this book. Some growers think its usefulness is a myth while others think it's an essential process that creates the best buds for smoking and vaporizing.

There are many reasons to question the efficacy of flushing:

1. Eliminating or lowering the availability of essential nutrients slows growth at all stages, including the last weeks of flowering.

2. It is difficult to flush large plants that are grown in bags containing 200-300 gallons (760-1140 l) of planting mix. The plants' roots have a reservoir of nutrients to draw from. Yet, these plants are savored by connoisseurs.

3. There are no double blind studies that have been performed to test the efficacy of flushing.

4. Although certain stresses increase trichome production, it is doubtful that nutrient deficiency is one of them. Trichome and oil

Left: [Photo by David Downs @True Humboldt Farms]

production is expensive; it requires the plant to expend energy. It seems counter-intuitive that depriving nutrients would increase cannabinoid/terpene production.

5. Some gardens using perpetual harvest techniques as well as aquaponic grow methods have no provision for flushing but produce fine connoisseur buds.

6. Large amounts of Calcium (Ca), one of the mobile nutrients, are required for cell division. To mature, plants must grow new cells. Without a constant supply maturation slows.

Only a small amount of Boron (B), another mobile nutrient, is required for plant growth. Without it in sufficient quantities bud maturation slows or stops. So, long flushing periods are likely to reduce yields.

Despite the lack of peer-reviewed studies regarding efficacy, the overwhelming majority of marijuana growers flush. The consensus is that depriving plants of nutrients during the last phases of flowering results in a higher quality bud.

FLUSHING METHODS

There are a multitude of flushing methods but they share a common goal: to remove most of the nutrients available to the roots, thereby encouraging the plant to use the non-assimilated salts it is holding.

The result is the plants will hold few nutrients in their raw form, and instead incorporate them into their tissues or into phyto-chemicals released by the roots.

In order for roots to absorb nutrients, the nutrients must be dissolved in water. Nutrients that are precipitated, either of a solution or bound in a molecular matrix, are not available to the roots even if they are plentiful.

Flushing with water rinses out the nutrients that are already in the solution. To rinse, use tepid water (about 75° F/ 24° C) that is adjusted to a pH of about 5.8-6.0, which is the range at which the nutrients are all soluble. With warmer water flushing, more nutrients dissolve and rinse away. The more you rinse, the more nutrients will be carried away. Nitrogen is the most soluble nutrient and it is the most likely to affect flowering negatively. Even using a rinse that drains only 10% of the added water removes some of the nutrients.

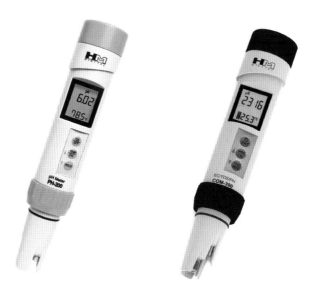

pH, EC and TDS meters are essential tools required to properly adjust water nutrient solutions. When the pH is out of suggested range (that is, too high or too low) nutrients fall out of the solution and precipitate. Plants drink their nutrients rather than eat them, so nutrients that are precipitated are not available to them. The pH must be adjusted for the nutrients to dissolve again. Above are two meters from HM Digital: The PH-200 (left) is a professional grade pH/ Temp meter ideal for all pH testing. With an advanced microprocessor and ATC (Automatic Temperature Compensation) it provides highly accurate, dependable readings The COM 300 (right) is a handy combo meter that measures pH/EC/TDS/TEMP. Both are waterproof for durablility.

As the flush continues, the PPM of the rinse water drops. This process can be stopped at any time. By leaving some nitrogen in the media, the plant still has some resources for growth, without the abundance that promotes vegetative growth.

Check the PPM of dissolved solids using a meter for both the soil and the water. With larger gardens, it may be more efficient to use just a few plants for trials.

Some techniques to consider:

- Some growers encourage vigorous vegetative growth before the plant makes a total switch to flowering. If doing so, leave the plants unflushed, or even supply a small amount of nitrogen during the first two weeks of flowering and let it deplete naturally.
- Start with a passive flush, that is, let the plants use the reserves in the mix. Then perform an active flush close to ripening.
- Perform a constant flush. Each time the plants are irrigated, add enough water so 10-20% of it drains. The drain water will be rich in nutrients, so there is little salt build-up in the medium. There are few excess nutrients to flush near ripening.

pH

The solubility of the nutrients in the planting mix is pH dependent. The salts, that is, the nutrients soluble in flush water, are adjusted to 5.8-6 pH. It removes more nutrients than water that is not pH-adjusted.

Water Temperature

Salts are more soluble in warmer water. Adjust flush water temperature to 75° F (24° C) if possible. More nutrients will be flushed.

Extreme Over Fertilization

Extreme over fertilization results when the water solution outside the plant is more concentrated with fertilizer and nutrient additives than the solution within the plant. The outside solution draws water from the plant which quickly wilts and then dries out.

Sometimes drowning roots resulting from an anaerobic solution is mistaken for over fertilization because drowning roots cause leaves to "weep" much like the leaves of a weeping willow; however "drowning" roots don't dry out the plant.

FLUSHING TECHNIQUES

Marijuana growers use a variety of flushing theories and techniques. There is no one correct technique. Just because it isn't mentioned here, doesn't mean it isn't helpful.

Flushing techniques can be divided into three main categories: passive, active and chemically-enhanced.

PASSIVE AND ACTIVE FLUSHING

The difference between passive and active flushing is that at some point in the plant's rush to ripening, either the caretaker or nature makes a decision to help the plant ripen by removing nutrients from the soil. The primary nutrient that is removed in this process is N, although many other water-soluble nutrients are removed.

Left: An example of nitrogen deficiency. The fan leaves are turning yellow. This plant was receiving too much flowering formula and was over-watered.

Plants growing in mix or soil are flushed using water. Dissolved and soluble salts are drained out. Depending on how thorough the flush, much, most, or nearly all of the soluble nutrients are removed. They are often replaced with a new flowering formula that may contain some macro or micro fertilizers as well as hormones, enzymes or sugars.

Plants react quickly to this sudden change in the environment by focusing their energy on maturation of flowers rather than continued production of flowers.

PASSIVE FLUSHING

Most modern marijuana plants ripen 7-9 weeks after being forced to flower. Their planting media may include ingredients that gradually release nutrients and is often irrigated using a water/nutrient solution. If the planting media is composed of the usual ingredients such as peat moss, coir, or compost, its copious carbon-containing molecules bind some of these nutrients and is ready to release them when nutrient levels get low.

Depending on the size of the plant and container, the media type and the technique being used, this process can take up to three weeks. Irrigate with nutrient-free water so no new nutrients are provided for the last 1-3 weeks of flowering. For instance, a nine-week plant won't be fed after the sixth, seventh or eighth week of flowering.

The theory behind flushing is: if nutrients are unavailable to the roots, the plant turns inward to find them. This works with large plants as well as small ones. In order to determine the quantity of nutrients needed to flush a plant, you'll first need to calculate the cubic volume of the container.

When actively flushing nutrients from a container using water, the rule of thumb is to flush with approximately 20% of the container's cubic volume 2-3 times throughout the course of a 7 to 10 day period. Doing so will deplete the media of its available nutrients by midseason.

Left: A vegetative plant with N deficiency. When N is lacking, the mobile nutrient is transferred to the canopy where it is most effective. The bottom leaves lacking N turn yellow.

However, enriched organic soils and planting media, especially if they have been used for more than one season, are likely to contain organically locked nutrients that mycorrhizae and other rhizosphere organisms will immediately begin to unlock; this provides more nutrients to the roots.

Then, as the residual nutrients are used up, the plant taps into its own reserves. Some of the minerals are mobile— nitrogen (N), phosphorous (P), potassium (K), magnesium (Mg), molybdenum (Mo)—and they translocate to the canopy top, where new growth is happening and where the plant's energy provider, the lights or the sun, is available.

As the leaves lose N and Mg they turn yellow. The loss of P and K results in leaf edge curl and dead spots. After the plant has extracted the valuable nutrients from the leaf, leaving mostly cellulose, it has no further use and it withers and dies.

These are indications that the flushing is working. The goal is to time the total loss of nutrients with ripening of the buds so nutrient deprivation does not cause appreciable loss.

Calcium (Ca), sulfur (S), iron (Fe), boron (B) and copper (Cu) are immobile and their deficiency symptoms, which usually don't occur in late flowering, can be seen in the new growth. Iron (Fe) deficiency, though rare, often results in bright yellow leaves around the buds. But the same effect could also be caused by N deficiency late in flowering. Lack of Zn, which is rare, causes twisted atypical growth.

As the leaves dry the buds continue to grow and mature. They use the reserves being drawn from the media, roots, xylem and leaves.

Flowering formula fertilizers contain little or no N. Plants growing in soil or planting mixes use the residual N loosely bound in the media that continues to dissolve. The major nutrient N, which is mobile, translocates from the lower leaves to the upper canopy. The lower leaves turn bright yellow then curl and dry. Hydroponic mixes without media reserves require some N during the first half of flowering (usually 3-4 weeks) and less during the next quarter (10-15 days). The lack of N towards the end of flowering hastens ripening and maturity. This is one of the cues the plant uses to begin ripening.

Flushing Time Recommendations by Media

▶ **Clay Loam: 15- 20 days.**

SOILS:

▶ **Sandy Soil: Flush for a week. It doesn't contain very much organic matter to bind the nutrients and it rinses readily.**

▶ **Porous Loam: Flush for 10-15 days. Some nutrients are held tenuously to the matrix and need a bit more flushing than sandy soils.**

▶ **Heavy Loams and Clays: Flush for 15-20 days. These soils bind nutrients that are hard to rinse away and must be used up by the plant.**

▶ **Enriched Soils and Mixes: Soils that were enriched using additives such as plant meals and manures may not require any flushing. Soil microorganisms dissolve the nutrients locked in organic compounds and provide them to the roots as needed. Most nutrients that are left are still locked up in organic matter. There is probably very little free N. However, if bottom leaves are not yellowing, there is too much nutrient left in the soil and the mix should be flushed.**

▶ **Planting Mixes: Planting mixes differ in their abilities to buffer or hold nutrients so each should be dealt with in its own manner.**

▶ **Peat moss and Coco: Flush one week if bottom leaves are green and 3-4 days if they are yellow. These mediums buffer nutrients (nutrients attach to them), but flushing will have a noticeable effect on the crop. The free nutrients are already dissolved and are easily rinsed away.**

▶ **Medium-free/Hydroponic Systems (aeroponic, deep water culture and some nutrient film techniques): Flush 3-4 days. As soon as the water/nutrient solution is removed and replaced with pH'd water, the roots have no access to nutrients. The plants react immediately, first showing signs in the lower leaves, which turn yellow. The buds also ripen faster.**

▶ **Medium-based hydroponic and fertigation systems (drip irrigation, ebb and flow, wick, capillary mat, reservoir, manually irrigated nutrient/water): Flush 4-7 days. The roots in these systems are usually anchored in a non-nutritive mix composed mostly of coir or peat moss. Infrequently, clay pebbles or perlite are used. None of these bind tightly to the nutrients so plants respond immediately to the new nutrient-free environment.**

COMMERCIAL FLUSHES

Flushes remove or make nutrients unavailable to the roots so plants are forced to use their reserves for growth. The free nutrients that were in the xylem or dissolved in the extracellular water bind to molecules in the plant's bio-system, creating a smoother draw.

The most popular flush is plain water. Salts in the media or in hydroponic units are all water soluble, or they're precipitated, that is, have dropped out of the solution. Precipitated nutrients cannot be taken up or used by the roots. Other salts are bound to larger organic molecules attached to the planting medium. These are only moderately available to the roots and are made available through mycorrhizae and other organisms in the rhizosphere (the area of the media that surrounds the roots). All other salts are soluble and drain out when flushed.

A few flushes claim that they contain chelates that actually draw nutrients from the plants. This may be true but has not been proven yet.

Once plants are flushed they draw from nutrients within their systems. First they use the unbound nutrients held in the xylem and the extracellular water channels. Then the mobile nutrients, nitrogen (N), phosphorus (P), potassium (K) and magnesium (Mg) migrate from the lower parts of the plant to the canopy that is getting light. A large light unobstructed plant will deliver nutrients to the sunlit sides as well as the top of the plant. Rather than only going up, the nutrients travel out, to the growing tips and maturing flowers. The immobile nutrients, boron, calcium, copper, iron, manganese and zinc remain stationary. Chlorophyll and other mineral-laden organelles in the cells break apart, facilitating the migration of the minerals they contain to the most active areas of the plant. Lacking the macro-nutrients, these leaves lose their green color created by Mg, turn yellow or tan and dry up.

Popular Commercial Flushes

PRODUCT NAME	COMPANY	INGREDIENTS
Clearex	Botanicare	Electrolytes in water
Flora Kleen	General Hydroponics	Nutrients unidentifiable
Final Flush	Gro-Tek	CITRIC ACID, ASCORBIC ACID
Royal Flush	Humboldt Nutrients	25% polyloxy-(1,2-Ethanediyl), Used in cleaning products and hair dyes-suspected endocrine interruptor, Alpha (nonylphenyl), Omega-Hydroxypoly (oxyethylene-iodine complex)

▶ **Clearex by Botanicare : The citric acid dissolves free salts in the rhizosphere. The simple sugars help provide the plants energy for growth via the mycorrhizae.**

▶ **Flora Kleen by General Hydroponics: Contains dilute acids which dissolve both precipitated salts in the system and around the roots**

▶ **Final Flush by Advanced Nutrients: Citric and ascorbic acid. Flavored varieties are sometimes artificially colored and flavored using synthetic dyes and flavors.**

▶ **Flawless Finish (MgSO4) by Advanced Nutrients: May have some unlisted ingredients, probably amino acids that chelate salts making them unavailable to the roots.**

▶ **Heavy Finish by Heavy 16: The humic acid makes some salts more soluble and the acids dissolve and bind some of the nutrients, making them easier to flush.**

▶ **Madfarmers Detox by Mad Farmer: Unspecified acids dissolve and bind salts so they are unavailable to the plant. The fulvic acid may make the salts more soluble and easier to flush away.**

▶ **Sledgehammer by Bush Doctor: Saponins is a natural soap-like substance derived from yucca.. It lifts and unbinds the salts making them easier to flush away.**

Garden Profile: SPARC
San Francisco, California

MARKET: Medical
SIZE: 500 lights
LIGHTING: Indoor HPS, 1000w
MEDIUM: Hydroponic
YIELD: 5.5 annual harvests, total of 22 harvests a year

The goal of the garden is to provide SPARC's busy downtown San Francisco dispensary with 14 strains grown in-house and to be an industry leader in new genetics, consistency, quality and safe growing practices. SPARC has a policy of not using petroleum-based products or growth hormones in the garden.

The garden is constantly growing a rotation of strains to meet the varietal demands of the market. One of the biggest challenges the garden faces is syncing the needs of patients with cultivation timelines and harvest schedules. Strains are chosen for smell, potency, flowering times and ability to thrive in SPARC's standardized practices as well as genetic resistance to pests, diseases and light stress.

Plants are grown to about 2-4 feet (0.6-1.2 m) tall. Their nutrient needs are met with ionic salt and root drenches. The perfect day to harvest is determined toward the end of flowering through daily monitoring of trichomes to assess both ripeness and cannabinoid content. The plants are flushed for two weeks and receive 48 hours of darkness before they are harvested.

During the last five days of the flush, the large fan leaves are stripped from the plant. Each strain is harvested individually. Workers cut the remaining branches of buds and sugar leaves from the main stem and inspect them before transporting them to the drying and curing area. The buds are dried on food-grade slotted racks with temperatures around 62-65° F (16-18° C) and relative humidity set between 52 and 56%. Buds are fully dried and cured before they are trimmed.

Buds are trimmed by hand to retain higher trichome levels and bag appeal. Moldy buds are disposed of and not sold to patients. SPARC's advice for other growers? Document the results for each strain grown. Share knowledge with others to improve the industry, and stay away from short-cut products such as petroleum-based sprays and growth hormones. Keep the consumer safe; the best cultivators are the cleanest cultivators.

[Photos by David Downs @SPARC]

6

Ripening

CANNABIS IS A SHORT-DAY plant. It measures the length of uninterrupted darkness chemically to determine when it is time to flower. To do so, it produces pigments called phytochromes that have active and inactive forms. They are kept inactive by the presence of red light in the spectrum of 640-680 nm. This occurs all day long. At night, when the light is no longer present, phytochrome gradually becomes active. As the length of the dark period increases, the phytochrome builds to a critical level, forcing the plant to flower. Each strain has its own hard-wired program that determines the duration of the dark period needed to create enough active phytochrome for flowering to occur. This is why varieties start to flower at different times.

Cannabis strains other than auto-flowering varieties follow the same general pattern. As latitude increases, the length of the growing season shortens. For the most success evolutionarily, plants should grow as long as possible vegetatively, leaving time to flower and develop mature seeds before they die from bad weather. As a result, plants adapted to high latitudes require fewer hours of darkness to initiate flowering than varieties adapted to lower latitudes.

Indicas and kushes are early-season plants that flower in mid-summer. They evolved at the 35th parallel north, in the Himalayan foothills, and have a shorter growing season as compared with equatorial sativas, which evolved at the equator. Sativas often initiate flowering in September and have a longer time to flower and mature than do Indicas.

[Photo by Doobie Duck]

Ask Ed: How can I get my plants to ripen faster?

Increasing the dark period from 12 hours daily to 13 hours signals the plant to stop growing flowers and instead to ripen up. The plants also respond to nutrients. They initiate ripening, in part, when they are deprived of nitrogen (N), which causes them to redistribute the N from their lower leaves to the buds.

DISRUPTING THE PHOTOPERIOD

There are a number of reasons for using the photoperiod to alter cannabis' usual flowering pattern.

Problem: In warm parts of the country such as the southern tier the temperature is warm enough and the light adequate to support growth in late winter, but the day length is short. Without altering the light the plants would immediately start to flower.

Solution: In order to maintain vegetative growth and discourage flowering too early the dark period must be interrupted. Break up the night cycle with short bursts of light so the plants never receive more than 4 hours of uninterrupted darkness. lluminate the plants several times a night. "Spraying" all parts of the plant with light for a short period, stops the plants from initiating flowering. When the plants receive red light or light that contains red, such as light emitted by warm white, 680 nm red fluorescents or HPS lamps, they reset their count of the critical time period.

Problem: Often it is beneficial to ripen a crop quickly early. Plants that ripen early in the season avoid problematic weather changes in the fall. In addition, the light is brighter and the UV light more intense, resulting in higher potency.

Solution: Use light deprivation techniques to limit the length of light time. This forces the plants to flower

Indoor growers and growers using light deprivation outdoors usually use a regimen of 12 hours of uninterrupted darkness each day, although most varieties will switch to flowering under a shorter dark regimen. A 12-hour light regimen is only a rough guide to inducing flowering.

Calculating the Critical Dark Period

Oscillating lamp mounted above the garden was turned on for a few minutes every 2 hours in the spring to interrupt the dark period. This prevented the plants from flowering.

A leisurely walk nightly at 1 AM with fluorescents mounted on a pole interrupted the dark period. White fluorescents emit light containing a red spectrum that restarts the dark count.

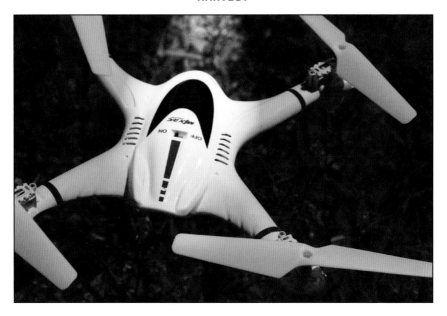

A drone controlled by a GPS program can be used to effectively deliver lighting for regulating plant flowering.

Take this specific example: on August 15 the day length in Oregon or New York (43.8° N) is 15 hours and the dark period is 9 hours. Most indica-dominant varieties display signs of flower initiation. Since they take about a week of critical dark period to indicate flowering, it can be assumed they were first affected by the critical dark period on August 8, when there were only 8.5 hours of darkness. Varieties usually vary in critical darkness requirements by about 8-11 hours.

Knowing this critical time period can be very useful for both indoor and outdoor gardeners. Indoors, growers can keep the lights on for longer periods during early flowering. A longer day length will result in more growth. Only as the plants reach their fourth or fifth week of flowering is the light period reduced by another hour or so to induce ripening.

Outdoors, growers can schedule light deprivation curtains for shorter periods so plants can get more sun for growth and still be forced to flower early.

Aside from the photoperiod, several other factors affect flowering time:

- **Intensity of Light:** Light is the energy that fuels photosynthesis. The brighter the light, the faster the plants mature. When plants receive suboptimal light levels, their growth rates slow and total yield decreases.
- **Nutrients:** The more nitrogen (N) that plants receive in late flowering, the longer they take to ripen. The more potassium (K) they get, the faster they ripen.
- **Temperature:** Photosynthesis and plant metabolism are affected by temperature. High temperatures hasten ripening; low temperatures prolong time to maturity. Plants function faster when leaf temperature is higher, about 80-86° F (27-30° C). However, the plant goes into stress mode and stops photosynthesizing at about 90° F (32° C).
- **Ripening Patterns:** Some varieties mature all at once, so the whole plant can be picked. Other varieties mature from the top down. Buds on the outside of a branch mature faster than inner buds hidden from light. Top buds often mature before lower ones.
- **Weather Conditions:** Picking is also determined by seasonal conditions that vary from year to year. Seasonal variations can shift ripening back or forward about 10 days.

ENVIRONMENTAL PRESSURES

Indoors

Indoors, where environmental conditions such as temperature and humidity are controlled, growers face few environmental challenges leading up to flowering and ripening.

The main challenge is often timing. While the current crop is flowering, the crop right behind it is being prepared for flowering.

When the newest crop, still in the vegetative stage, is growing too fast or getting too large, the solution is to slow its growth. This can be achieved by changing the environment. The three factors that primarily determine growth rate are light, temperature and nutrients. Dimming the lights, lowering temperatures to the mid 60s (around 18° C) and lowering the nutrient levels affect the growth rate of plants profoundly. They will remain healthy but will hardly grow. The plants will start to grow vigorously again only when the environmental conditions change to bright lights, higher temperatures and more nutrients.

Outdoors

Growers face picking pressures caused by improperly planning for environmental factors.

Sunny, warm, dry weather is ideal for ripening and harvesting. The sun, powering photosynthesis, provides energy for ripening. The warm weather promotes fast growth, and with little moisture there is less chance that powdery mildew or other infections will occur.

Gardens often have those conditions all summer long, but in autumn the plants are in a tug of war with nature, ripening just as conditions get more challenging. Light intensity and UV light levels are diminishing, and it may be cloudy, foggy or rainy—all perilous environmental conditions.

Growers must contend with autumn's rapidly changing climate. A common challenge outdoor grower's face are buds that won't be ready for another 10 days, but the forecast is for several days of cool, damp or rainy weather, followed by sunny weather. That's when growers face the conundrum: harvest before ripening or risk the bad weather?

WET HARVEST

Harvesting in fog or rain presents special problems because wet vegetation is vulnerable to attack by bacteria and mold. In this situation, prepare the plants or branches by hanging them or placing them on drying racks, leaving more space than usual to promote drying. Raise the temperature to the mid-70s and circulate the air while removing moisture using a dehumidifier or room dryer. This will lower the risk of infection and decrease drying time.

You can use a hairdryer, leaf blower, or an outdoor space heater to dry live wet buds. Once they have dried resume your normal drying techniques.

If the fog lifts or the rain stops and is replaced by sunny weather, postpone harvest until the plants have dried.

PREPARING FOR BAD WEATHER

As the crop ripens, monitor the weather forecasts for at least two weeks before planned picking. Take the forecasts into consideration when selecting harvest dates.

Depending on the weather conditions, growers may choose to harvest, protect the plants with covers or tarps, use drying equipment and/or spray with protectants. Usually large-scale outdoor growers proceed cautiously. They choose not to risk the whole crop to botrytis just to gain a slightly higher percentage of THC. Moisture is a problem with dense, thick buds that are more prone to mold than fluffy or thin bud strains.

If the indoor or light deprivation greenhouse harvest must be picked early and there is sufficient warning, speed up ripening by increasing the dark period to 14 hours daily. This induces the plants to ripen faster at the cost of bud size. Turning off the light a day or two before harvesting also helps a little with ripening and may increase THC/terpene content. Keep temperatures in the low 70's (around 21C) and the humidity below 50% in the dark space to prevent mold infections.

Some possible ameliorative actions can be taken in the midst of a crisis:

- Keep rain off the plants to prevent the mold that grows when inner portions of the buds capture water. Cover the plants with a tarp, or if they are in moveable containers relocate them to a greenhouse or indoor grow area.
- Once the rain or fog stops, use fans and heaters with warm, not hot, air to dry the plants and buds.

Fog is not healthy for buds. Prevent mold by spraying with 10% milk solution or 1% potassium bicarbonate before fog or after rain. [Photo by David Downs]

- Spray with a fungicide approved for use on edible crops. Organic OMRI-listed organic fungicides such as Ed Rosenthal's Zero Tolerance™ are approved for organic grows. A solution of water and 10% milk and 1% potassium bicarbonate can also be used to control fungal infections naturally. Portable UVC lights such as Aeon Clean Light kill fungal spores before they germinate. An alkaline pH on the leaf surface prevents spore germination. Spray with water adjusted to about pH 9.

If the forecast reports nasty weather for an extended period of time, it is not worth the risk to leave the plants unharvested. Picking immature buds is better than risking their ruin.

Several methods can be employed to prevent this problem in future gardens:

Raindrops push their way into bud crevices where they create moist conditions ideal for molds and bacteria. Placing a tarp over the plants prevents this penetration. Large fans can be used to dry the buds quickly after rain. [Photo by David Downs]

Pulling tarp over plants towards the end of day. The dark period is extended to 12 hours, forcing the plants to flower.

- Use strains that flower and ripen early to avoid the threat of bad weather. Choices include early flowering and auto-flowering varieties.
- Use light deprivation. By shortening the day length to 12 or 13 hours, or the number of hours that your variety of plant needs to initiate flowering, the plants are forced to flower early. If they are covered daily starting on June 20, most varieties will ripen by August 15, before autumn weather and while visible light and UV light are still intense.
- When growing indicas or indica hybrids in lower latitudes, night interruption may be the best practice to keep plants vegetative, even during summer months. As soon as these lights are turned off, the plants will indicate.

BENEFICIAL MYCOS AND BACTERIA

Mycorrhizae are mushroom family organisms that form beneficial and symbiotic relationships with plant roots. They are part of the rhizosphere, the matrix surrounding the roots. They make it easier for plants to obtain nutrients as they protect it from pathogens. By helping the plant deal with the environment and mitigate stress throughout its life, they increase the plant's vitality and yield at harvest.

PRODUCT NAME **Bloom Enhancers**	COMPANY	INGREDIENTS
Floralicious Bloom	General Hydroponics	General Hydro, humic acids
Rainbow Mix Bloom	Earth Juice	Earth Juice, Mycorrhizae, humic acid
FloraNectar	General Hydroponics	$MgSO_4$, $k2SO_4$, secret ingredient - probably simple sugar
FloraRush	General Hydroponics	$MgSO_4$, $k2SO_4$, secret ingredient- probably simple sugar, perhaps synthetic flavor/aroma
Black Pearl	Gro-Tek	N-P-K, soluble kelp extract, charcoal
Bloom Fuel	Gro-Tek	$K2SO_4$, humic acids
Bloom Blaster	Gro-Tek	$KH2PO_4$
Heavy Bloom	Gro-Tek	$KH2PO_4$, KNO_3
Monster Bloom	Gro-Tek	$KH2PO_4$, $MGSO_4$
Purple Max Snow Storm	Humboldt County's Own	Triacontinol (stimulates faster growth rates by increasing the number of basel breaks, increasing root growth and flower size)
Snow Storm	Humboldt County's Own	Triacontinol
Massive Bloom	Green Label	N-P-K, Amino Acids, Vit. B1, B2, Triacontinol Carbohydrates, humic acid Full chelated micros, Mg
Ginormous	Humboldt Nutrients	$P2O_5$, $K2O$, unspecified micro-nutrients
Bloom Master	Earth Juice	$KH2PO_4$, Kelp, p, naturally occurring minerals, phyto-acids, N,P and K compounds, citric acid, guano, steamed bone meal.
Ionic PK Boost	Growth Technology	P.K. NIPACIDE Formaldehyde based biocide. (Used industrially. Not used for food products. Toxic.)

Roots Organics Buddha Bloom is a hydroponic plant nutrient solution made from a blend of organic bat guano, worm castings, kelp extract, molasses, yucca extract, and humic acid. It can be used from the early flowering stage through harvest.

Bloom Master
Earth Juice Bloom Master is a concentrated, water-soluble plant food supplement specifically formulated to promote vigor, increase yields and enhance quality in plants during the flowering stage of their life.

STANDOUT BLOOM ENHANCERS

Because blooming plants need more nutrients (particularly phosphorus and potassium) to stimulate growth and flowering, growers often administer products such as bloom enhancers or stimulators. I have had good experience with the following products in enhancing my harvest.

- **Buddha Bloom:** A good combination of natural ingredients
- **Amino-Aide:** Contains amino acids that promote increased flower growth
- **Big Swell:** A good combination of ingredients; promotes growth, contains nutrients and sweetener
- **Zyme:** Contains the catalyst amylase, that turns starches into sugars, sweetening the buds
- **T-Rex:** Contains growth proteins that also promote branching
- **Purple Max Snow Storm:** Contains natural plant growth stimulators Triacontinol and Jasmonic acid that increase yields
- **Snow Storm:** Contains growth stimulator Triacontinol. Increases yield
- **Sugar Peak Grand Finale:** A good combination of natural ingredients that promote growth and sweetness
- **Bloom Master:** A good combination of ingredients. Natural plant nutrients that promote growth in early-mid flowering
- **Massive Bloom:** Contains Triacontinol, amino acids and excellent combination of nutrients that promote growth in early to mid flowering
- **Bud Factor X:** Contains Chitosan, which promotes SAR response, promoting vigor, stress resistance and growth

- **Big Bud:** Contains amino acids, flowering nutrients and plant hormones that promote flower growth
- **Nirvana:** An excellent combination of natural ingredients including hormones that promote growth and flowering
- **Terpinator:** No ingredients listed. CANNOT make a determination without ingredients

UNACCEPTABLE BLOOM ENHANCERS

- **Cutting Edge Bloom:** Uses Paraben
- **Ionic PK Boost:** Uses Nipacide

BUD SWEETENERS

If using molasses or another sugar in the water/nutrient mix, continue using it throughout ripening, even when flushing. One formula is 1 tsp/gallon (5 ml/4 L) or a tbsp/5 gallons (14 ml/19 L) of water.

Each of the products that were listed has an effect on the taste and the form of the buds. Unfortunately, there have not been side-by-side controlled tests so you have to rely on you own experience and those of others who have shared theirs' in garden forums.

THE RIPENING PROCESS

Knowing when to pick a ripe bud is as much art as science. Each grower has their own processes and criteria for determining ripeness; but there are a number of things a savvy grower will watch for. Most follow these steps:

Indoors, most growers induce their plants to flower using twelve hours of uninterrupted darkness. However, plants can be forced to flower at a shorter period of darkness. Outdoors, look for the first signs of flowering and then count back one week from that period. Look online for dusk and dawn hours in your region. Count the number of hours between dusk and dawn; that is the number of hours it takes to force flowering.

Once a plant is forced to flower, it takes between seven and nine weeks for it to ripen. Let's go through some of the stages of ripening during this period.

Huckleberry Kush Sugar Leaf Tip [Photo by Professor P @ Dynasty Genetics]

HARVEST

During the first week of flowering you'll see the beginning of stigmas. Stigmas are white hairs that protrude from the newly-forming pistils. They're hollow inside and have brushes on the outside through which they filter the air containing pollen. When they capture the proper grain of pollen, they strip the sperm from the pollen and send it down the hollow tube to meet the egg. If the stigmas are unpollinated they remain white for a long time.

By week four the plants are in full flower and they put out layer after layer of stigmas so the bud gets thicker and thicker and eventually, quite hard.

By week six the buds start to ripen and the stigmas start turning brown. When growing outdoors, the days get shorter and the nights become longer. The trichomes, the glands on the leaves surrounding the flower that hold the THC and other cannabinoids and terpenes, start becoming more prominent; eventually the caps on these glands start filling up.

By week 7 or 8 wre're about a week away from ripening. Most of the stigmas are brown and the trichomes are more prominent. The glands continue to fill up with THC and terpenes; they look like mushroom caps. They begin to bulge like balloons. The odor becomes more intense; but the bud is still not ripe. It still hasn't reached peak intensity.

This is a ripe bud. You can see that the trichomes are totally erect and the caps on them are prominent. They're bulging with resin, the stigmas are brown and in this case a fake seed pod is visible. This isn't unusual. Fake seed pods can develop with some varieties.

Now let's look at it close up. These are all mature flowers. You can see the caps are bulging, but at this stage you see that almost all the glands are clear but a few are beginning to change color, either to an amber color or to a milky white. That's an indication that they're changing from potent THC to much less potent CBN. It's at this point that the plants should be picked. This period lasts about 72 hours, depending on the variety.

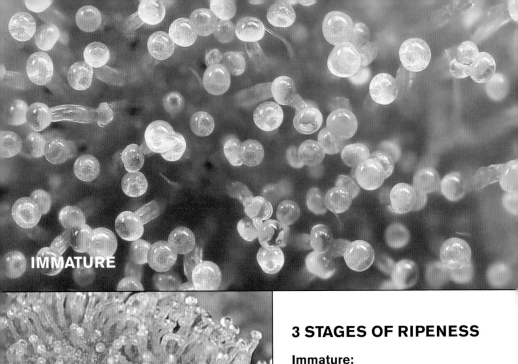

IMMATURE

IMMATURE

3 STAGES OF RIPENESS

Immature:

The trichomes are filled but the caps are not bulging. They are all clear and the odor is beginning to increase. In the last week the intensity of the odor will quadrouple. When completely filled the caps will look like balloons ready to burst. [Top & Bottom Photo by Professor P/Dynasty genetics]

MATURE

Mature:

The trichome caps are bulging. The vast majority remain clear but a few have changed color to white or amber, indicating a change of THC to CBN, a less psychoactive cannabinoid. The odor has increased and reached peak intensity.

MATURE

OVERRIPE

Overripe:

As the buds grow stale the odor becomes less pleasant—s smell somewhat akin to fermentation. The glands turn color indicating change of THC to less potent cannabinoids, and the gland heads start falling off the stalks.

Picking

ONCE THE GROWER DETERMINES the buds are ripe, it is time to pick.

STEPS TO PICKING

1. **Inspect for ripeness:** Regularly examine buds for signs of ripening.

2. **Plan:** Estimate the date the buds will first be ready to pick. Schedule time and resources for picking.

3. **Trim:** If convenient, about three weeks before ripening, begin removing fan leaves that aren't getting light or are blocking buds from direct contact with the sun. Remove other fan leaves a week to a few days before harvest.

4. **Flush:** Begin the flushing regimen about 15 days before ripening.

5. **Disinfect the processing and drying/curing areas:** Clean all surfaces and tools with alcohol or disinfectant.

6. **Prepare:** Ready the tools, equipment and drying area. Clean and inspect all equipment to make sure it is working. Tune up tools by sharpening, oiling and charging them. Make sure there are enough tarps and baskets and an area large enough to store the harvest.

7. **Cut:** Remove buds when they have reached peak potency. Alternatively, cut entire branches of buds the same length for easier processing. Make sure to cut branch ends at a blunt, 90-degree angle. Sharp 45-degree-angled branch ends puncture storage bags. Do not touch, shake, tear or drop the buds.

8. **Remove excess leaves:** Trimming excess leaves shortens drying

Cutting branches at True Humboldt Farms. [Photo by David Downs]

time. If convenient, pluck the large fan leaves from below the buds. Fan leaves often snap off when the plants are freshly picked and still filled with water. Fresh, "wet" vegetation is turgid and easy to handle. The trichomes that hold cannabinoids and terpenes are pliable rather than brittle and more likely to stay attached to the plant. When dry, the glands can snap off when the buds are handled. To keep trimmed fan leaves fresh for making juice, extracts and concentrates, place them in a cooler with ice as they are picked.

Another method is to leave the fan leaves on the cola. Drying takes longer, but the leaves protect the buds. This step facilitates the process when trimming is planned after drying.

9. **Sort:** Gently place picked buds or cut branches in trays for transfer to the trimming or drying area.

To capture the greatest amount of THC and terpenes, plants should be harvested toward the end of the dark period. If the garden is outdoors, the best time is before sunrise. If the garden is indoors, it is best to leave the lights off during the harvesting process and pick after the plants have gone through a full dark period. THC and terpenes accumulate during that time, so an extended period of darkness produces the most THC.

PICKING STYLES

Growers have many choices of how to harvest. Here are some different styles.

Whole Plant

There are several reasons for cutting the whole plant at once:

- The buds have matured at the same time. This often happens on small plants or when the entire plant is fully illuminated. All the buds on sea-of-green plants usually mature at the same time.
- Weather conditions are threatening.
- The entire plant, or most of it, is to be used for extracts or concentrates, so full cosmetic ripening is not important.
- Space needs to be made for new planting. If the planting area is scheduled to be replanted, waiting for some buds to ripen throws off the schedule. It is usually not worth the time delay.

Pros: The plants are quickly removed from the field or room and away from environmental stresses

Cons: Not all the buds are perfectly ripe. Some are either over-ripe or immature and are best used for concentrates and extracts.

Top: A feshly cut plant is taken from the room in Colorado and then tagged. It will be tracked through to sale. After tagging, the plants are hung on moveable racks and brought to the drying room.
Bottom: Buds dry slowly in a drying room, kept at about 55% RH at a temperature of around 70°. [@Green Man Cannabis]

Branches

There are several reasons to cut branches as they ripen:

- Cutting branches may be more convenient than cutting the whole plant.
- On outdoor plants, the budded portions of branches usually extend no more than 2 feet (0.6 m) and rarely beyond 3 feet (.9 m). Removing just the budded parts of branches leaves behind extraneous vegetation.
- A large plant may be too heavy and bulky to cut at the stem so it has to be taken down in pieces.
- One side of a plant, usually the south facing, which gets more direct sunlight, often ripens first. Removing these mature branches opens up inner buds to direct light.
- Some branches may be in the shadow of other plants or other obstructions, especially in autumn, when the sun's angle is oblique. Removing ripe branches often allows light to reach the other branches.

Pros: There is a greater selection of ripeness. Because growers are dealing with less bulky vegetative material, they can more easily manage and process it. They can also better utilize smaller spaces.

Cons: More time is spent in the field cutting branches.

PREVIOUS PAGE: A mature plant ready for cutting.

TOP LEFT: The branch is cut just below the node where it meets the stem.

BOTTOM LEFT: Another branch is cut.

RIGHT: The branches are easily bunched for transporting.
[Photos by David Downs]

Whole Ripe Buds

Some outdoor growers choose to pick individual buds as they ripen. This may be an advantage for large as well as small operations because it extends the harvest period so a smaller team is employed for a longer time. Some of the reasons using for this technique include:

- Cutting just the buds eliminates processing a lot of bulk vegetation that has little value.
- Less space is needed in the drying and curing areas.
- Less labor is required after cutting.
- Growers can ensure that every bud is at peak ripeness.

Pros: Harvesting individual buds as they ripen gives lower buds hidden inside the canopy the chance to fully mature in another 5 to 10 days. There is a significant difference in potency and quality between unripe and ripe buds, so the extra time and labor required for multiple harvesting sessions or daily bud inspections are well worthwhile, even for large harvests. Another advantage is that the most valuable buds are removed first, and therefore safeguarded. The inner buds are not nearly as valuable.

Cons: Harvesting whole buds takes more time and labor than cutting whole plants or branches. Some training is needed to recognize ripeness.

Ripe Portions of Buds

Many buds ripen first at their tips and the ripeness travels inward. One portion of the bud may be ripe while the other portion is not. For perfection, the ripe portion can be harvested and the inner portion will receive more light as it ripens.

Water Deprivation

Experienced growers practice slight water deprivation 1 to 2 days before harvest. This creates a stress response so that more cannabinoids and terpenes are produced. The deprivation should not be so severe that it leads to wilting.

First the large fan leaves are trimmed off giving easier access to the bud.

LATE PICKING

Sometimes crops are harvested late. The main indications are that the caps on top of the trichomes have changed color from clear to amber or milky white as the THC changed to CBN. Some of them have popped off their stalks. There is no way to reverse the change or to improve the potency of late, degraded bud.

Picking Indoors

Cool the room to 70º F (21º C) and lower than 50% humidity. The cooler temperature keeps the terpenes from evaporating, and the low humidity minimizes the threat of mold. Use bright non-glare lights to illuminate trim stations. Overhead, floor lamps and desk lamps provide good light.

Picking Outdoors

Outdoors, where maximum size or height might not be much of an issue, huge plants can be harvested two or three times by taking the ripened portion of each bud and leaving the unripened portions to finish over the next week or two.

Outdoor growers have no control over temperature, humidity and wind. Ideal conditions for picking are cool and dry, less than 70º F (21º C) and low humidity. In reality, poor weather may require an early harvest. The best time to harvest is before dawn or early morning, when the plants contain the most terpenes.

Plants grown using a sea-of-green method have a single layer of tops because very little light pierces the canopy. Vegetation below the canopy can be used for concentrates. On the other side of the spectrum, monster plants spaced farther apart absorb light over their entire height. Some varieties ripen uniformly. Others ripen top down.

Weather also affects ripening time. The southern sides of the plants ripen first in cool weather; plants with low levels of nutrients ripen later. Dryer soil or planting medium decreases time to ripening.

Medium and large-scale growers should use a system to provide individual plant attention and at the same to attend to the needs of the entire crop. There are two possible paths, depending on the growing conditions and the grower's needs: a slow, elongated period of harvesting or one big harvest. Most indoor farms use the former, while outdoor operations use the latter.

Growers who harvest all at once should plan for staff. Think of it as a snake swallowing large prey. There is a surge of work all at once followed by digestion, which can be accomplished in a burst or over a longer period.

Massive outdoor plants usually are harvested in one or two cuts. The best flowers are harvested for their buds; the rest, consisting of small, immature or late flowers and leaves, are used for extract.

Another strategy eliminates the need for a temporary labor surge. First, all labor is devoted to harvesting. Plants are cut and hung to dry or are placed in a refrigerated space where they remain fresh for processing. Then, they are processed over time.

When only a single variety is grown, all of the plants ripen at the same time. If labor is limited, cutting only buds or bud parts that are ripe paces the work. These buds are processed as the next group ripens. During the growth cycle, fertilization is easier because the same formula is used for all the plants at the same time.

Space is another factor to consider. Continual production of small harvests is less likely to max out the drying, curing, trimming and storage areas.

EQUIPMENT USED FOR HARVESTING

- **Tarps:** place around large plants when cutting them.
- **Shelves or hang lines:** hold whole plants, branches, colas or buds.
- **Transporting equipment:** moves material from field to processing. This may be a basket or a hand-drawn garden cart, small motorized transport or a portable conveyor belt.
- **Cool room:** keeps the buds cool and turgid while awaiting processing or, alternatively, a drying room.
- **Photographer's loupe or a magnifier:** monitors terpene progression and ripeness.
- **Schedules:** keep track of the entire process and manage various important factors and tasks.
- **Cleaning supplies:** including vacuum cleaners, brooms, dustpans, alcohol and hydrogen peroxide, clean rags, paper towels, soap and water, resin removers such as potassium hydroxide (KOH) or commercial resin solvents. Workers should practice proper hygiene, and washing facilities should be available.
- **Gloves:** for all phases of the operation, from plant cutting to manicuring. Canvas, rubber and latex gloves are among the choices.
- **Clippers or power cutters**

Gloves coveredd in Hash [Photo by David Downs]

- **Food-grade plastic trays:** hold material for sorting fan leaves, branches, colas, trim, buds and trash.
- **Ergonomically correct tables and chairs.**
- **Solvent:** such as isopropyl alcohol, olive oil, or commercial resin degreaser to clean resin off scissors and other surfaces.

Find a good pair of gloves

Find comfortable gloves that do not impede work. Thin cotton gardening gloves protect the skin for jobs such as moving branches. When handling larger plants and thick branches, use more protective gloves. Garden gloves are a good choice for handling buds and small branches. Be sure to choose the right size—they should fit the trimmers' hands snugly; it is difficult to work with loose gloves. After manicuring, trimmers often put gloves in the freezer to easily peel the hash that collects on them.

MANUAL CUTTING TOOLS

Choose tools based on ease of use, comfortability, and how well they work. Below is a range of trimmers—small and large, long and short-handled—as well as a sense of what to look for in a high quality trimming tool.

Hand Trimmers

The garden section of your local hardware store likely has three kinds of hand tools useful for picking cannabis—bypass, anvil and ratchet tools.

Bypass: A bypass cutting tool works by sliding a straight blade past another blade. The bypass cutter's scissor-like motion works well for cutting live green plants. The firm outer wall of the plant yields easily to this bypass motion. Bypass cutters have a stainless steel curved blade on the bottom of the tool and a straight blade on top. The straight blade passes next to, not on top of the lower surface, sometimes called the hook. The lower blade's curvature is designed to hold the branch or stem while the cutting blade descends and cuts. Bypass cutters

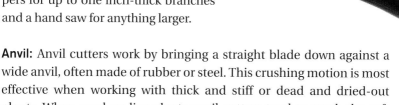

offer a very clean cut because the blade slices all the way through the plant material. Use bypass pruners for up to three quarters of an inch-thick branches, bypass loppers for up to one inch-thick branches and a hand saw for anything larger.

Anvil: Anvil cutters work by bringing a straight blade down against a wide anvil, often made of rubber or steel. This crushing motion is most effective when working with thick and stiff or dead and dried-out plants. When used on live plants anvil cutters tend to crush the soft tissue of the plant, stopping the flow of nutrients and prolonging the

healing time for the cut surface. An anvil cutter dulls less quickly than a bypass cutter and can't be damaged when twisting the tool in the cut, as can happen with bypass cutters.

Ratchet: Ratchet pruners are used to cut thick branches or stalks. They are either hydraulic or pneumatically driven. One handle is stationary and the other moves. The lower jaw of the pruner hooks around a stalk or branch when the handle is pumped. As the blade sinks into the material the ratchet gear clicks into place. The user then continues the pumping motion until the cut is complete.

Small pruning saw: When a branch or stem is too large or unwieldy to make a clean cut with a cutter or a lopper tool, you may elect to use a small pruning saw. There are two types of pruning saws—straight and curved blade. As the name indicates, straight blade pruning saws have straight blades. Though the blades are straight, the handles are often curved, like a pistol grip, making it more comfortable to use. Straight blade pruning saws are best used for green plant material.

Loppers: The long handles of a lopper allow you to extend your reach with minimal effort, enabling the user to cut anything that can fit between the two blades.

Curved blades are best for heavy-duty cutting. The curvature of the blade allows the user to add additional force to the cut, slicing through even the toughest branches and stalks. But using a pruning saw or lopper takes time; when working with large plants growers should consider electric tools to increase efficiency.

A hedge trimmer with an 18" cutting area allows cutters to reach tall branches and to reach into bushy plants. They can be directed very accurately to remove individual buds as well as branches.

POWER TRIMMERS AND CLIPPERS

Use of portable electric tools speed up the process of cutting buds considerably, by a factor of 3-8 times the pace of manual work. Electric hand garden trimmers often come with two different blades that facilitate precision work. They can be used when leafing. They are useful when harvesting small plants or buds, or even just the ripe portion of the buds, leaving the unripe portions. Each of the two blades are small, usually a hedge trimmer about 5-8 inches (12-20 cm) long and a grass shearer about 3-4 inch (7-10 cm) wide. Depending on the bud formation and plant shape, both of these cutters can be used to remove the ripe buds from the plant, leaving the unripe buds or just the branches and the leaves from which the buds stuck out.

Versions of these tools come with pole extensions up to 10 feet (3 m), so tall plants can be trimmed while the worker stands on the ground rather than on a ladder or platform. This is an important issue because workers are more likely to sustain an injury when working while elevated.

The buds were cut from this 6.5' tall plant in just a couple of minutes. Only the stem and inner portion of the branches were left standing.

Large Hedge Trimmers

When removing branches it is often easiest to use a hedge trimmer. They can also be used to harvest buds or remove just the ripe parts of buds.

Hedge trimmers have blades that are 12-24 inches (30-60 cm) long. Smaller trimmers are adequate for most plants and weigh less than models with longer blades, so workers don't tire as quickly.

If the branches are too thick for the trimmer to handle efficiently, either use a reciprocating saw or small chain saw. Look for lightweight models that are easy to wield overhead but rugged enough to handle the work.

Harvesting time decreases 50 to 80% when power hand trimmers, hedge trimmers and power saws are used. A plant that would take 15 to 30 minutes to cut with hand tools can be cut in 5 minutes or less using power tools.

Plants growing in a Christmas tree formation can be harvested with five strokes. There are four columns of branches, one on each side. Lay a clean tarp down to catch the cut branches. Starting at the top branches on one side of the plant, begin cutting near the node, where the branch meets the stem, bringing the trimmer down the length of the plant. All of the branches will fall into a neat pile on the tarp. Move to each side consecutively. Then cut the top. The buds on the branches will be the same size and equal length; only the bare portions of the branches will differ in length. The branches will collect in neat piles because the buds aren't touched while cutting.

Bushy plants and plants with multiple branches are also easy to cut using a hedge trimmer. A giant plant that takes 15 to 25 minutes to cut using hand tools falls to the trimmer in a few minutes. Using power tools results in less contact and thus, less damage.

Afterward, either the tarps containing the buds can be rolled up or the buds can be placed in containers. Then they should be quickly moved to a cool area for processing.

Depending on the distance from the field or grow room to the next station, a simple garden utility cart, an electric utility vehicle or motorized transport such as a golf cart may be practical.

At this point there are two avenues a grower may choose: trim while the plants are wet or when they are dry. Each has its advantages and disadvantages. (See more in Trimming.)

The inner branches contain no buds and very few leaves. Rather than sorting it later, the operator selected only the budded colas for harvest. A tarp was laid around the plant to catch the falling buds. When the cutting area is done the tarp is pulled away from the plant, folded into a bundle and transported to the processing area.

Since the buds are not touched during the cutting process, and are soft and pliant because they are fresh rather than dried, they suffer little damage from exposure to the vibration of power tools.

This photo series started with the low branches already removed. The rest of the plant was cut to the ground in less than 60 seconds. Compared to cutting by hand, there is less damage to the buds. A tarp placed underneath the plant makes it easy to gather the harvest and move it to the processing area—a 5 to 10 minute process completed in less than 2 minutes.

Battery Operated Shears [Zip Snip]

A small, battery operated rotary saw with a safety switch; the guard/guide limits the size of the stems it can cut. Removing a portion of it lets it tackle bigger jobs. This is a precision tool excellent for removing leaves several days before harvest, hand pruning buds or just collecting their ripe parts. A comfortable grip and lack of pressure helps prevernt carpel tunnel syndrome. [Photos by Darcy Thompson]

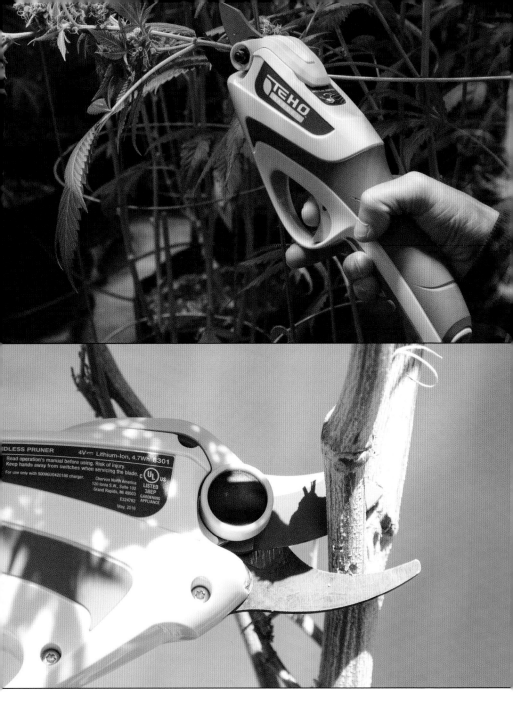

Battery Operated Shears

Electric clippers do the work, eliminating strained muscles and carpel tunnel syndrome.

Battery Operated Trimmer

A hand held, battery operated trimmer is useful for removing large leaves and exposing the buds, making more precise trimming easier.

Mini Hedge Trimmers

The Efficient Way to Cut Buds from Plants with Mini Hedge Trimmers

- *Place a tarp under the plant to catch all the buds or branches that are about to fall. Start with the vegetation closest to the ground and cut the buds along the stem upward. They will fall off the plant in much the same way that hair drops when it is cut. Work up the plant in an orderly manner. If the buds are too tall to reach, use a secure step stool to increase reach. With the right equipment, workers should be able to easily cut the buds from a plant 8-10 feet (2.4-3.0 m) tall.*
- *Small hedge trimmers are most useful for cutting small branches and individual buds. They work very well on bushy plants. The buds from a garden of sea-of-green plants are easy to harvest using these tools. When the trim has been completed, the plant will still look green but bereft of buds, or will hold only immature buds left to ripen.*

RIGHT PAGE TOP: Bovine transport cart, Khandwa India [1981]

RIGHT PAGE BOTTOM: Hand toting crop from the field, Switzerland [2000]

TRANSPORTATION

Depending on the size of the crop and the distance the buds or branches need to travel to be cleaned, processed and cured, a variety of transportation methods can be used. The simplest method involves transporting trimmed buds in bags or sacks. For bigger grows, where the quantity of material increases and efficiency becomes a greater factor, often carts, trucks or conveyor belts are used.

TOP: Handcart @ SPARC Garden [2016]

BOTTOM: Utility Cart, Tahoe CA [2008]

TOP: *Flatbed Truck, Australian Outback [2006]*

BOTTOM: *The SmartFlo system of WPS, The Netherlands, consists of several modules of conveyors that are connected online. The SmartFlo Flexit, one of the essential elements of SmartFlo, is a flexible conveyor belt that is easy to install and relocate. [2017]*

CLEANING OUTDOOR CROPS

Sanitation is something to watch as testing requirements become more common. Prevent contamination by using tarps to keep plants from touching the ground. Keep dust to a minimum by spraying down dusty gardens before beginning harvesting.

After picking, some outdoor growers clean their crops with hydrogen peroxide. When the plants are growing in a windy environment, the sticky resins trap and hold dust, dirt and bacteria from the air. Both indoors and out, powdery mildew infections can cover a plant. Mix standard hydrogen peroxide (typical store-bought hydrogen peroxide is a 3% solution) with 200-250ml or about 8oz in 5 gallons of water to create a hydrogen peroxide bath. If the hydrogen peroxide used is greater or less than a 3% solution, adjust your water ratio up or down accordingly.

Dip the freshly cut branches in the solution. Some growers soak branches for up to 30 minutes. The water will turn a muddy color but will not strip the branches of trichomes or chlorophyll, only the dirt. Immediately set the washed material out to dry. Hanging is best. Use fans to quicken the process. If hydrogen peroxide is unavailable a similar cleaning technique can be employed by mixing a ¼ cup of lemon juice and a ½ cup of baking soda in 3.5 gallons of water.

Some ways to keep dust to a minimum:

- Outdoors, moisten paths and unpaved roads.
- Inside drying spaces use air cleaners with UVC lights enclosed that capture particles in filters. The UVC lights kill airborne spores and bacteria.
- Filter incoming air. Particulate filters remove the larger particles. Carbon filters clean the circulating air. They keep the smell down inside the room.
- Keep the surfaces "restaurant clean" by wiping down tables, chairs, prep areas, floors and entranceways with hydrogen peroxide.
- Keep a wet/dry vacuum handy for use in cleaning debris and messes.
- Cover picked material to prevent it from picking up dust during transport to drying or processing areas.

Large scale indoor cutting @Bolder Cannabis [Photo by David Downs]

Hygiene Rules

1. Use best sanitation practices: wash hands, use hygenic gloves, sweep debris, and clean work area after each project. Everything–tools, cleaning equipment, storage boxes–should have its own space and be labeled with procedure for use, if necessary.

   Do the same thing for outgoing material. Everything should be sorted and marked.

2. Process the harvest in a different area than the growing space to avoid contamination by workers and their clothing or tools.

3. No pets should be allowed into the growing or processing areas.

8

Trimming

TRIMMING IS THE PREPARATION of the bud after it has been cut from the plant. How and when buds are trimmed depends on the grower's goals and strategy. The purpose of trimming is to separate the highest-quality part of the plant, the ripe female flowers (buds), from the stems and leaves. Manicuring is the final step in the trimming process and is a skilled task that requires training and experience.

Trimming should not be confused with pruning, which is the removal of unwanted vegetation from living plants, including weak branches, leaves below the canopy and vegetation hidden from direct light.

PARTS TO BE TRIMMED

The bud is the cannabis plant's jewel. It is a clutch of flowers that continue to grow for 6 to 12 weeks. The flowers squeeze tightly between and on top of one another, forming thick layers, until the entire group is a dense floral mass.

More than one bud grows on each branch. If buds grow large enough, they grow into each other forming one continuous group called a "cola." It is always found on the outer extremity of the branch. The branch usually grows at nearly a 90° angle to the plant's stem, although branches of some varieties may curve upward. Trimming starts with the removal of the branches from the main stem. From that point, the order of the trimming process varies greatly, but to create a fully manicured bud:

- The bud is clipped from the branch or cola.
- The fan leaves are removed.
- The trim leaves surrounding the buds are removed.
- Any extraneous material is removed.

What's left is the manicured bud. Fan leaves contain small amounts of cannabinoids, and trim leaves contain a larger amount. Both are usually saved either for use or sale for extractions and concentrates.

TRIMMING STYLES AND STRATEGIES

There are many ways to trim. Style and method depend on quantity and quality of the crop, goals and personal preferences. The biggest difference is between wet and dry trimming. This refers to the condition of the harvest, whether the material still contains the moisture it had as a living plant or whether it has been dried. The process—whether trimming and then drying, or the reverse—requires preparation. The complexity of planning increases with the size of the crop.

De-leafing is the removal of the large fan leaves shortly before harvesting. Removal opens up the plant so sunlight can reach the buds. This enables the buds to grow and ripen faster and develop more potency. Later, harvesting is easier without the bulky leaves.

In the Field: Wet vs. Dry Trimming

Most growers of large outdoor crops use a combination of wet and dry trimming. They must prepare a temporary space, since it's used only once or twice year, and have the time or people to cut and handle the harvest. Meanwhile, the trimmer or trimmers are cutting as fast as they can. Sometimes available labor is overwhelmed and plants or branches are hung to dry. However, with increasing popularity of trimming machines more buds are trimmed wet.

Growers with indoor and greenhouse gardens, where harvesting is year-round, also tend to manicure wet. It is a routine that requires time and space; whether the garden is run by one person or is a large enterprise, space and labor are set aside specifically for trimming tasks.

A hygenic bud preparation and packaging area. People are wearing gloves but should also be wearing hairnets. [Photos by David Downs @Boulder Cannabis]

Top Left: Clipping off the last of the large fan leaves. [Photo by David Downs]

Top Right: Then the smaller trim leaves surrounding the bud are removed.
[Photo by David Downs]

Bottom Left: The trimmed buds are cut from the stem. [Photo by David Downs]

Bottom Right: The buds are placed to portable nylon net drying racks that are
are easy to install and remove. The buds are drying in single layers about 2"
thick. They breathe from both top and bottom because of the open netting.
The space's temperature and humidity are controlled automatically.
[Photo by Justin Cannabis]

Wet Trimming

Wet trimming is a sticky, time consuming process, but it is popular with growers who are concerned with processing their harvest quickly or have limited space to dry their crop. The process of trimming wet bud takes longer, but if a grower has an entire team of people standing by, she/he may not have the luxury of waiting for the entire crop to dry.

If you have a lot of material to process or don't have a lot of manpower, then a wet trim is probably the safer option. If quality is your main priority and you have sufficient manpower then a dry trim is recommended.

PROS

- A naked bud takes less time to dry than does a bud surrounded by leaves.
- Buds are dried in trays and on screens, which take less space than hanging whole stems.
- Wet trichomes are more pliant, so fewer snap off.
- Wet hand trimming produces plentiful "finger hash:" hashish that is ready to be smoked right off workers' gloves or hands.
- The crop is processed as soon as it is cut and is ready once dried and cured.
- Wet trimmed buds often have a "tidier" appearance than dry trimmed buds.

CONS

- Wet hand trimming is slower than dry trimming because the wet plant is pliant and harder to cut.
- In surge situations, the crew may need to be temporarily enlarged to trim the buds before they wilt.

Top Left: Sativa bud has a lot of fan and trim leaves surrounding it. These leaves are being pulled off by hand. [Photo by David Downs]

Top Right: Next the leaves closest to the bud are pruned with scissors. [Photo by David Downs]

Bottom Left: The bud is cut from the stem [Photo by David Downs]

Bottom Right: A bud being finished by hand over a screen. Trichomes knocked off the bud fall through the screen and are later collected as kief, which is often pressed into hash. The bright light results in less eye-strain and higher quality work. Worker should be wearing gloves.

Right Page: The Trimbag is perhaps the simplest way to manicure dry bud. Place five lbs. of dried un-manicured buds removed from branches in the bag and shake for five minutes. The buds and leaves are separated and then the buds are picked out from the bed of trim.

Dry trimming

Dry trimming is more popular than wet with some producers, because dried buds are stiffer and easier to cut and handle but dry trichomes are brittle and break off easily during trimming. Collect them using screens and trays. This powder, called kief, can be smoked, sprinkled over bowls and into joints, pressed into hash or used for processing into extract.

PROS
- Dry trimming is faster and easier than wet trimming. Rather than using scissors, gloved hands simply snap off the dried brittle leaves.
- Surge harvesting is processed more easily. The only tasks essential to the harvest are to cut the buds, colas or whole plants and provide them the proper environmental conditions to dry. A small crew trims for a longer period after the harvest.
  - Buds can be trimmed anytime they are dry. There is no immediate need for large crews working around the clock.

CONS
- Buds allowed to dry on the stems with leaves attached dry more slowly and take up more space than buds manicured wet and dried on screens.

- More trichomes are lost to handling. Once the trichomes are dry and become brittle, they fall off buds more easily.

Whole Plant Trimming

Some growers trim plants hanging upside down when they are wet or dry.

Place a tarp on the floor to catch the trim. Starting at the top (the bottom of the plant), trim away everything but the best buds. Leaves and immature buds are quickly stripped off the branch using a canvas-gloved hand. Then clip off the buds for manicuring.

Left: Trimming fresh indoor plants on the line. While the plants are still turgid they are hung upside down at a comfortable height to work while standing.

Right: Using clippers both the fan and trim leaves are removed leaving just the trimmed bud on the branches. The buds are clipped off after the plants are removed from the line.

Trimming Tips

▶ **Separate the processes of stripping, bucking (removing the buds) and trimming. This maximizes efficiency. Personnel can be switched between activities as needed.**

▶ **Break buds along their natural structure and reduce stems to imperceptibility. Buds should be no bigger than 3-4 inches (7-10 cm) in diameter.**

▶ **Move the bud, not the scissors. Roll the bud in the hand to best angle it into the blades, which are held steady at the same location and angle.**

▶ **Look for mold or mildew. Diseased leaves are a sign of infection. The biggest, most dense and often most beautiful buds are most susceptible to mold.**

Do Not Under-water!

TIP: Do not try to save drying time by under-watering plants at the end of their life. Hand processing limp buds is frustrating work. The branch can't be held upright; it leans, making it difficult to pluck or cut fan leaves. Leaves don't snap off as they do when the branch or cola is turgid. When the plant is limp, trimmers often hold the branch the worst possible way: by the bud.

HOW TO HAND TRIM:

1. Install a clean table and adjustable-height chairs that comfortably place trimmers over the table or use a trimming tray that sits on the lap.

2. Use gloves at all times.

3. Place a screen under the trimming area to collect trichomes. Trichomes fall off constantly during handling. Capture them using framed silkscreen or stainless steel mesh. Prefabricated screens are available online or are easily made with a 100-micron-thick mesh fastened to a frame.

4. Disinfect transport bins and tools with hydrogen peroxide or alcohol. This helps prevent bacterial proliferation.

5. Arrange separate bins for midgrade buds and for top buds, all other saleable buds, extractable material and trash. Only the top buds need to be manicured. The other material will be sold or used for processing.

6. Clip off the popcorn buds (also called larf). Place them in their own bin.

7. Then trim the smaller, multi-fingered leaves surrounding the buds. They are called sugar leaves, or trim leaves. They are also clipped off.

8. The bud should now appear almost naked, except for some single-fingered leaves sticking out from between the flowers as well as the few sugar leaves for protection. Watch out for buds that are much bigger than the others. They take longer to finish drying and are more susceptible to mold. They can be dried separately or broken down into smaller buds.

9. Collect trichomes from the table or trim bin.

10. Scrape finger hash from scissors.

11. Clean up.

USEFUL TRIMMING TOOLS

Keep Your Blades Clean

With increased use, trimming shears and scissors acquire plant resins and become too sticky to cut. Trimmers use a variety of around-the-home substances to keep blades clear, including commercial products such as olive

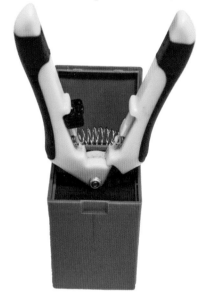

oil, vegetable oils and isopropyl alcohol. Keep cups near scissors to soak them or dip them before scrubbing off the excess hash.

*Trim scissors parked in a **Scissor Scrubber**. The Scissor Scrubber holds the oil or alcohol in a spill-proof container that allows the trimmer to quickly dip and scrub the blades in one action while the lid squeegees off the excess. The bristles won't dull the scissor's blades and are easily removed for cleaning. [Photo by Darcy Thompson]*

Use a Professional Work Surface

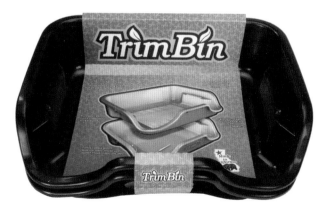

*The **TrimBin** by Harvest-More is sturdy and ergonomically designed to sit atop the worker's lap. It is simple, easy to carry, easy to clean, and promotes organization with various compartments to hold tools. Buds sit atop a stainless steel screen so trichomes are collected in the plate underneath.*

Workers processing buds. The fellow on the left has an allergy to marijuana so he works covered with a respirator. He should not be working in this environment because there is always the chance of accidental contact. During certain times of the day there is sufficient sunlight to create a bright environment conducive to precision work. During mornings and late afternoons work stations should have better illumination. [Photo by David Downs @Bolder]

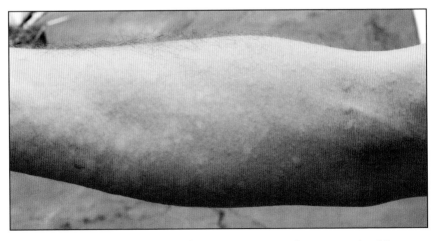

A rash from marijuana exposure during processing. This person should not be working close to marijuana. The rash is an inflammation on the skin. Who knows what's happening internally? Don't play with your health.

BEST PRACTICES

Safety & Comfort

Wear gloves, work clothes, appropriate footwear and goggles when using power equipment. When working near noisy equipment, wear noise filters or headphones that block noise but allow communication with mics and speakers.

Long hair should always be tied back and covered with a hat or netting.

High pressure sodium (HPS) lights, which emit the amber light often used in indoor grow spaces, are not suitable for use in the trim room because they may be uncomfortable for trimmers, distort the image, and slow the work pace.

The best light to use is: filtered sunlight coming through windows, skylights or greenhouses; overhead LEDs or fluorescent lights with a color of about 5,000 kelvin (very similar to sunlight); or table, floor, reading or workstation lamps that direct light onto the stage where the work is taking place.

Workers should take a break every two hours or less and they should not miss bathroom breaks or meals. Water and other hydration should be available and close by at all times.

Most standard water hoses used in gardens make potable water non-potable because they contain lead. All hoses used for drinking water should be certified for potable water.

Injuries from repetitive stress lead to chronic pain and permanent damage. Anyone who feels muscle stress or fatigue should be relieved of duty before they strain their muscles or sustain a more significant injury.

Worker Health

Anyone on the job who develops an allergic reaction to any part of the plant or its dust should not work on the site. An individual's health is worth more than a paycheck.

The most typical allergic reactions that are expressed physically are pimples or rashes, flushing and a hoarse voice. Much rarer symptoms that need emergency treatment are trouble breathing, feeling lightheaded or fainting. These symptoms are external manifestations of inflammation. Internally other body parts, including organs, may also be affected.

Late Trimming

Growers sometimes dry the buds, colas or whole plants, and trim only as the bud is used. This process minimizes disturbance to the trichomes. The extra vegetation takes longer to dry and cure, but the rush and frenzy of harvest is eliminated and workers, if needed, can be hired at the grower's convenience after the demand for labor has subsided. Make sure to keep the storage area humidity at about 65%. Plants kept in an area that is too humid are subject to mold.

Hiring Workers

Hire and schedule trimmers. Use personal references and interview each about their relevant experience. Always test the trimmer. Inefficient and negligent trimmers can ruin high-grade cannabis flowers and cost far more than they are worth. Slow trimmers slow the pace of production of faster trimmers who often adjust to a slower pace.

The health and safety of workers is the grower's responsibility. Long-term repetitive work, such as hand trimming, can lead to repetitive stress injuries. It is imperative that trim stations be ergonomic.

Trim Temperature

Trimming should be done at a clean, climate-controlled, comfortable trimming station. Keep the temperature at 65-70º F (18-21º C) to prevent terpene evaporation. Maintain humidity at about 50%. Workers might feel chilled – provide sweatshirts of different sizes.

Outdoors, trim when the temperature is cool rather than hot and with little wind so the buds aren't contaminated with dust. Don't leave plants, buds or trim in direct sunlight, which rapidly degrades cannabinoids. Use micro-emitters to cool the area and keep dust down by spraying dry soil.

Setting Up the Hand-Trim Station

- Light each workstation with bright, non-glaring light.
- Use comfortable chairs compatible with the job. They should help the operator face forward toward the work.
- Loud noise and interruptions disturb the workflow. The space should be fairly quiet, except for music, talk radio or recordings that all can agree on. If that's not possible, individuals should use earbuds.
- The space should be kept neat.
- Sweep and vacuum floors and sanitize surfaces frequently.

- Use carbon filters and air cleaners to keep the air dust-free.
- Trimmers should wear clean clothes and practice proper hygiene such as showering and hand washing. Shower space with clean towels should be available. Inform smelly people to clean up.
- Provide appropriate work gloves and hairnets.
- Trimmers should not be under the influence of alcohol when working. No hard drugs should be permitted on the premises.

Chairs and Tables

Chairs and tables affect productivity. View the chair and table as a unit. The chair should be adjustable in height as well as position so that the operator's back and shoulders are not hunched over and the arms are at a comfortable height, allowing the hands full mobility. Resin or plastic garden chairs do the exact opposite. Both the seat and the back force the body backward rather than toward the work. Office chairs used by typists are good choices. A jeweler's station is an ideal work area. Chairs made for handwork position the operator in a more comfortable, forward position. Lap trim trays are very popular because the operator can sit in a comfortable position with arms vertical from the shoulders rather than splayed out over a table. Trays work well but probably are not as efficient as a good chair-table unit.

The trimmer's body faces forward towards the work area. The table supports her arms. The light makes it easy to concentrate on detail. The shadow is a result of the camera flash.

Good Ergonomic Setup

A worker sitting at a workstation. The chair may be a little large to hold her sit bones firmly, but is designed to help her spine tilt slightly forward towards the work area. She is wearing gloves. A desk lamp illuminates the work well. She has enough space to organize her work. She should be wearing a hairnet.

What's wrong with this picture?

- The plastic resin chairs are designed to push the spine back away from the work. To compensate workers have to lean forward, tiring them.
- There is no table to use as a workstation.
- Both the untrimmed buds and the trimmed leaves are lying on the floor. Workers' shoes are actually stepping on some.
- The material is not organized into undone, trimmed and trim.
- Workers don't have any tools.
- Workers are not wearing gloves or hairnets.
- The space has only moderate ambient light. Brighter light focused on the work area would result in faster, higher quality processing.

VARIETIES OF TRIMMERS AND CLIPPERS

Bonsai Pruner, Bud and Leaf Trimmer

Squeezer steel scissors made before 74AD recovered from Pompeii. Since they were meant to be pushed in and then return to open position the metal had to be tempered. [Credit: Naples National Archeological Museum] A modern version manufactured in 2016. It is just 4 inches (10 cm) long with razor-sharp stainless steel blades, spring action and a delicate handle.

Wiss Clips

The Wiss Clip is a 4.75-inch (12 cm) stainless steel scissor with sharp-point blades that are replaceable. It has spring action and a heavy-duty contoured design with industrial PVC plastic handles.

Fiskars

Fiskars have a spring-action, symmetrical, soft-grip handle that works with right and left-handed users. Scissors on left are among the most commonly used and the scissors on the right make cutting thicker branches a snap.

Chicamasa Curved Blade Sap Resistant Garden Scissors

Made of the highest-quality stainless steel with a true curved blade and sap-resistant Florin coating to prevent buildup.

HAND-HELD MACHINE TRIMMERS

Electric scissors save hands, wrists and arms from repetitive stress while maintaining much of the control and the gentleness of hand trimming. About a dozen different types of electrical scissors and clippers are on the market.

ADVANTAGES:
- Saves hands ■ Doesn't tire ■ Prevents repetitive injuries ■ Faster

DISADVANTAGES:
- There is a learning curve. Training is required.
- May not be as thorough as a hand trim.
- Machine trimmers require slightly more maintenance than scissors.
- The up-front cost is higher than for manual scissors.

Bonsai Hero LED

The operator is using a Bonsai Hero Handheld Electric Trimmer. It has two stationary blades and a double-edged swinging blade that is constantly functioning. The operator controls the cut but doesn't have to clip. The blade speed is adjustable, making up to six complete trips a second. After mastering a short learning curve, the operator can trim two to three times faster than manually.
Manufacturer also makes a consumer version: Testarossa. This makes hand trimming go on fast-forward speed. See the video on YouTube at "Bonsai Hero electric hand held trimmers v3."

The Magic Trimmer is an affordable, corded, rotary action, electrical hand trimmer that is used to buzz leaves down to about even with the bud cola. It won't reach in and clip a leaf base like a pair of Fiskars, but it speeds trimming. Use the trimmer in a cubicle because the trim flies off the bud. A little touch-up manicuring may be necessary after finishing because the Magic Trimmer can't poke inside the bud.

Wander Trimmer EZ Trim

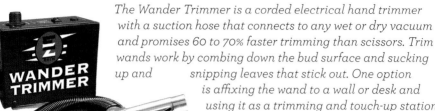

The Wander Trimmer is a corded electrical hand trimmer with a suction hose that connects to any wet or dry vacuum and promises 60 to 70% faster trimming than scissors. Trim wands work by combing down the bud surface and sucking up and snipping leaves that stick out. One option is affixing the wand to a wall or desk and using it as a trimming and touch-up station. The blades must be flushed with hot water hourly and cleaned daily. After many hours of use the blades dull and require sharpening.

BUCKING MACHINES

Bucking machines automate the process of removing buds from the stock. They can increase productivity by about 50%—some bucking machines can process up to 150 lbs of material per hour. To use a bucking machine, insert a branch into the appropriate sized hole. As soon as the branch is inserted, the bucker grabs it and pulls it through the machine, removing the buds from the stock. Bucking machines have variable speeds to process either wet or dry product. The machine can typically be cleaned with an alcohol spray or a pressure washer.

Bucking Machine by Greenbroz makes short work of removing buds from stems. The operator is feeding branches to the intake. The machine cuts bucking time down by two thirds and relives workers of repetitive labor that can cause injury.

A GreenBroz spinner machine in action.

MECHANIZE AND AUTOMATE

Every task involved with the harvest—cutting, trimming, drying and curing--has been affected by modern technology. Laborsaving devices are shortening the time it takes to perform each task. As growers, we must learn to adjust and plan accordingly.

Manicuring is a skilled but tedious task. Outdoors it is seasonal, creating bulges in demand for labor for a couple of months. Indoors, full-time, it is monotonous. In a high-powered, automated production system hand manicuring is an expensive, labor intensive anomaly. Professional manicurists trim 1-3 pounds (0.5-1.5 kg) a day. Almost all machines process 10 times that. Machines are quickly changing the economics of this portion of cannabis processing. When the first machines were released, cultivators faced the decision of using a machine that simplified processing and saved time and labor at the cost of some cosmetic loss. This is no longer as much of a consideration because newer models are gentler on the buds. Even the gentlest machine trim will result in some trichome loss on the surface of the bud; it's just a matter of how much. Remember, even the best human trimmers also lose surface glands. About 5% to 30% of surface trichomes are removed by machine trim.

Why Machine Trim?

Machine trimming makes sense for all growers no matter the size of the harvests. They can be used for all grades of flowers, including top-shelf.

Some machines handle top-shelf flowers better than all but the best hand trimmers. Machine trimming has been overly maligned, especially when taking into consideration that the work of human trimmers varies in both quantity and quality. Many trimmers do a lower quality trim at a far higher cost than a good machine. Even the best human trimmer tires after several hours, let alone several days or weeks on the job. By contrast, a well-maintained machine treats the millionth bud as nicely as the first.

Tight buds are the best candidates for automatic processing machines. The most common type of trimming machines are tumblers, which come in many models. The new models are very gentle and can trim even top-shelf material. The pitch or angle is adjusted, thereby slowing or speeding up the pace at which the buds tumble through the machine. Spending less time in the machine results in a "looser" trim, leaving on more of the tight trim leaf around the bud. Touch-up trimming is sometimes required, but the bud retains more of its trichomes with a loose trim.

Automating the manicuring of looser buds is best done using tools that assist the hand trimmer and are mostly operated electrically but are manually controlled. These tools use the operator's skill but eliminate the tediousness of scissors. Both small and large buds do well in manual and electrical spinners. The space and time savings of trimming wet with machines adds up quickly. Plants can be cut down with power tools and trimmed much more quickly with machine trimmers than is possible by hand.

Trimmers are usually designed to cut either wet or dry buds, although a few can process both. Before choosing, make a basic harvest plan.

The downside of machine trimming dried buds is that the buds are brittle, so trichomes snap off easily when manipulated. Dry trimmers are designed to capture trichomes that break off. Dry trimming machines have several different designs including tumblers and grill/slider models that don't move the buds around as much. Dry trim machine advocates say buds trimmed fully dry smell and taste better than buds trimmed wet; moisture may damage and degrade buds.

State regulations set thresholds on microbiological contamination of cannabis flowers and other products. Wet machine trimming may increase the likelihood of contamination because bacteria counts can build up in wet trimmers that are not cleaned and decontaminated regularly. Contamination spreads easily when the buds come in contact with bacteria. This is much less likely to happen when buds are trimmed dry.

Choosing the Right Trimming Machine

Aside from wet versus dry trimming capability, there are a number of other ways to differentiate machines.

- **Does the device assist the hand trimmer, or does it do the work?** Some examples: Bonzai Scissors (Trim-R-Matic), Magic Trimmer, Swingline Handheld, Trimpro Trim Box and Wander Trimmer assist the operator, replacing manual scissors in wet trimming.
- **Will the buds be cut wet or dry?** Grill-style trimmers are used for dry buds. The grill slides back and forth opening and closing; this movement catches and cuts the leaves from the bud, leaving them trimmed without much agitation. Cloth tumblers are designed for use with dried buds. The tumble gently agitates the leaves, causing them to break away from the buds.
- **How many workers does the device need?** The tumbler and spinner machines for wet buds do the trimming and the operators tend the machine, feeding it and removing finished product. The amount of production from these machines depends on the number of workers tending it.

Return on Investment

Some people see a large price tag on a machine trimmer and are put off. Don't think in dollars; think in pounds. A $3,000 machine is worth a few pounds of top-shelf trimmed buds and does the daily work of a team of hand trimmers. Just one day of using a machine trimmer generates a cost savings in labor as compared to hiring manual trimmers.

THE PLANT'S ROLE IN EFFECTIVE MACHINE TRIMMING

The plant's shape, density and moisture levels affect machines' performances. Dense buds sustain less damage than light, airy buds that have lots of peaks and valleys, or undeveloped larf buds.

Slow the machine's speed to trim airy buds. Dense buds with prominent sugar leaves can be trimmed at a faster speed without damage. The size of the load the machine is fed affects the trim. Test to see how large a load the trimmer can handle without overloading and damaging buds.

> ## Machine Trimming Tips
>
> ■ **Remove excessive stems and twigs before wet or dry trimming. Break apart big and asymmetrical buds.**
>
> ■ **Hang-dry plants destined for dry machine trimming. If they are dried on trays they will flatten out, making it difficult for machines to process.**
>
> ■ **Not all strains or all types of bud from a single strain are suitable for a single trimming machine. Loose, airy sativas are not as compatible with some models than are dense indicas and indica hybrids.**

Unlike the trimmer assist machines, which increase the speed that the trimmers are able to process bud, with tumblers and grates the processing speed is determined in large part by the number of people attending the machine. Aside from bucking, in which the buds are removed from the stem, up to five people can attend the machine, so the tumbler or grate is constantly processing. With fewer people, the machine may run empty.

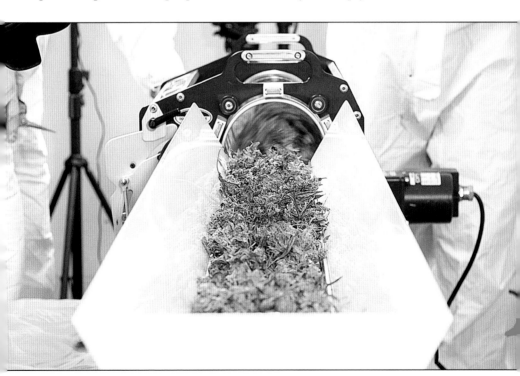

A KIERTON twister machine in action.

SMALL DRY TRIMMING MACHINES

GreenBroz Commercial Trimmer

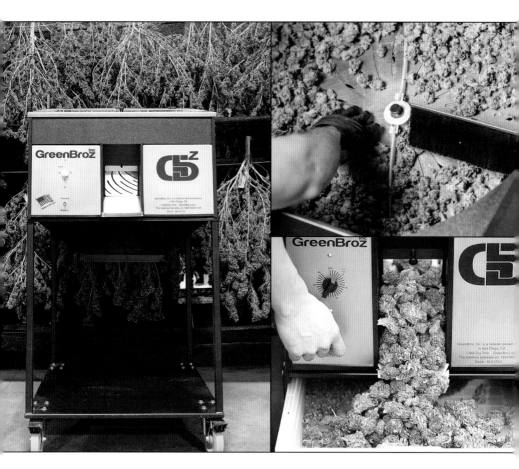

Left: The buds slide across a twisting grill that finishes the trimming and pop out the other end. The machines are variable speed, to adjust to the buds. They come in two models: Standard (215), which handles 2-4 pounds (1-1.8 kg) per hour and the Commercial (420) unit, which processes 8-12 pounds (3.6-5.5 kg) per hour.

Top Right: The GreenBroz 215 and 420 Commercial Dry Trimmers are tabletop units for finishing dried buds.

Bottom Right: Buds exiting the machine

Ultra Trimmer

An Ultra Trimmer processing dry buds.

Ultra Trimmer is a moving bed of stainless steel scissors that snips 4,872 times per minute with none of the harsh tumbling motions of similar units.

One or two technicians set buds on the scissors bed adjusting them during trimming and remove them when trimmed. This takes 10 to 15 seconds. The process is automated with an optional attachment. The machine can handle both dry and wet buds. The trimmings are ready for use in hash, and the machine comes with a removable drawer that separates different grades of extract material.

Like human trimmers, Ultra Trimmer handles rounded, dense strains better than larf. Ultra Trimmer comes in two sizes: 24 by 18 inches (61 by 46 cm) which trims 8-10 pounds (3.6-4.5 kg) per hour. The larger unit has a bed of 48 by 18 inches (122 by 46 cm) and trims 12-18 pounds (5.4-8 kg) per hour.

Tom's Tumble Trimmer

Tom's Tumble Trimmer uses gravity, not scissors, to trim 1-3 pounds (0.5 -1.5 kg) of material in 10 to 20 minutes. De-fanned, de-stemmed hang-dried buds are loaded into the zipper flap. The buds tumble over themselves and against the soft mesh netting, which breaks the leaves from the bud. The trim falls into a catch bag. The nylon net bags are treated to repel oil. The bags come with different size mesh tumbler screens as well as a kif screen for making trim. The screens attach with heavy duty velcro. Tom's has reasonably priced tabletop, midsize and large models, all with a heavy-duty motors and speed controls.

Close-up of Tom's Tumbler showing net that forms a drum.

Strategies for Using a Tumbler Machine

Personnel

The tumbler is turning. The rest is up to the attendees. It has to be fed; that requires one attendant. Someone has to provide the bucked buds for the filler to work. Then the buds exit the other side. Someone has to remove the collection basket and take it to the drying area.

Typical Outdoor Processing

This method requires a team of one to five people. With each added person the efficiency increases because the machine is working a greater percentage of the time.

- Bud sections of branches are cut and placed in bins.
- The bins are transported to the processing area.
- Using a 5-8-inch (12-20 cm) hedge trimmer attachment on a hand trimmer, buds are cut from the branches. They fall into another basket and are transported to a trimmer.
- Buds are fed into the tumbler and fall into a waiting basket.
- The basket is taken to the drying room and the buds are racked.

Method Two

This method requires a team of one to five people and works best if a machine is rented, borrowed or used collectively in a co-op.

- The branches or colas are cut from the plants and placed in bins.
- The buds are cut from the branches using the 5-8-inch (12-20 cm) hedge trimmer attachment on a hand trimmer and fall into another basket.
- The bins are transported to a room cooled to 40-45° F (4-7° C), where they are stored.
- All of the buds are bucked and ready to be processed. The tumbler is brought on site.
- Buds are fed into the tumbler and fall into a waiting basket.
- The basket is taken into the drying room and the buds are racked.

MEDIUM AND LARGE DRY TRIMMING MACHINES

Twister Trimmers

A twister's advantages include a very high throughput, quick handling time, a gentle tight trim, and a one-bud-in, one-bud-out flow. Buds aren't slamming into each other. Twisters trim both wet and dry flowers. Twisters are also modular; up to four units can be run in series for increased output and quality. Twisters come with a full three-year warranty. The biggest disadvantage to the Twister is that it is noisy. Ear protection should be worn.

Twister Tips

- Trim at 12% moisture, no more or less. Common moisture meters help ascertain the dampness of buds.
- Run the machine flat and slowly increase the angle to assess the results and determine the best angle for the specific job. Don't run too steep.
- Optimal feeding speeds vary by variety and environmental conditions. Test speeds and angles for each batch.

Kierton Twister Trimmer

Kierton Ind. produces a top of the line brand of commercial and industrial twister machines. Some of the options they offer are a hopper and a conveyor belt. The largest model, the T2, trims 35 wet pounds (16 kg) per houror 11 dry pounds (5 kg) per hour. A smaller model, the T4, trims 20 wet pounds (9 kg) per hour, or 7 dry pounds (3.2 kg) per hour. The newly-released T6 model is a small-capacity tabletop unit, with speeds of up to 4 pounds (1.8 kg) of dry bud per hour or 2 pounds (.9 kg) of wet bud per hour.

The Triminator

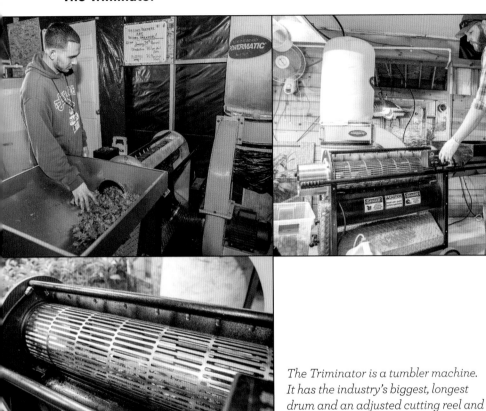

The Triminator is a tumbler machine. It has the industry's biggest, longest drum and an adjusted cutting reel and drum alignment that allows trimming to 0.0025 inches (0.06 mm). It can handle up to 20 pounds (9 kg) per hour.

The no-bed-knife design and self-cleaning mist system requires no lubrication. The belts and blades are 100% covered to prevent injury to users. We know of a few Triminator's that were used continuously without cleaning for days on end. In one instance a machine processed 800 pounds (363 kg) of material was processed. The Triminator Dry is an industrial level batch trimmer that loads quickly, is effortless to run and easy to clean. However, it is hard to move; and is not recommended for smaller harvests. Triminator Dry trims up to 8 pounds (3.6 kg) per hour with "set-and-forget" operation and no lubricants required, which keeps flowers and extracts pure.

Shearline Trimmer

Shearline makes small, medium and large wet trimmers in the classic shotgun barrel style. Bucked buds are loaded into Shearline's hopper. Press the on button and the hopper shakes buds into the trimming barrel. The vented barrel rotates over a set of cutting blades as a fan creates suction that pulls leaves through the barrel vents. Neatly trimmed buds tumble out of the barrel's end, ready to be rack-dried and cured.

Aside from harvesters and buckers, a recommended Shearline crew comprises four people: one person each to deliver buds to the area, feed the machine, remove processed bud from the machine and prepare the bud for drying.

Shearline uses distilled water mist inside of the machine and on the buds to prevent surface adhesion of super-sticky buds to the metal and to each other. The water evaporates during the trimming process

See more trimmers at *GrowersHouse.com.*

Troubleshooting

Early Harvest: If the harvest must be trimmed early in the season, there will be fewer mature, dense buds and more small buds and sugar leaves. If only a small percentage of the buds are grade A and most are loose, not only are they bad candidates for machine trimming because they will get sliced up in the trimmer, but they may not be worth trimming at all. They may be best used for making concentrates.

Lubricants and Anti-Sticking Agents

Some trimmers require lubrication of their cutting surfaces and moving parts. Cannabis resin is sticky and easily gums up machines, so any machine-trimmed cannabis will have some amount of residual oil on it. A few trimmers run without oil. A way to avoid contaminating the buds is to use an oil made specifically for the purpose.

Buds before and after trimming.

How to Buy a Quality Machine

- If possible, visually examine the quality of the material coming out of the machine and use lab tests to compare final potency of machine-trimmed material with hand-trimmed material.
- Read company brochures and ask for third-party analyses and testing reports.
- Check out Internet videos of the trimmer if they are available.
- Look at grower reports online.
- For peace of mind, buy from a company that's been in business for a few years. Compare warrantees.

Wet Trimming Tip

Keep plants cool, moist and turgid for the best machine trim. Hot plants get limp and gum up the machine. For the best results, trim wet in a climate-controlled (55° F [12° C]) room.

Garden Profile: Ganja Ma Garden
Laytonville, Mendocino County, California

MARKET: Medical
SIZE: 9,000 square feet (836 sq m)
LIGHTING: Sun
MEDIUM: Soil
YIELD: 2 pounds (1 k) per plant

Ganja Ma Garden provides a collective of patients with medical cannabis, with its ultimate goal being "spiritual upliftment and inspirational healing using sustainable methods." The garden is planted in the design of a Sri Yanta, a shape from sacred Hindu geometry. Ganja Ma is constantly studying and experimenting with natural methods and uses bio-dynamic techniques to grow the best medicine for the patients it serves.

Ganja Ma grows several local heritage varieties by working with some of the Emerald Triangle's top breeders such as Aficionado and TGA. It rotates genetics. Recently it has grown local strains such as Black Lime Reserve, In the Pines, Shakti and Orange Turbo. It uses "intuition and destiny" to select varieties to grow.

Before providing the garden with nutrients, they conduct soil tests to determine how to appropriately amend the soil, using Grower's Secret soy-based fertilizer. Although Swami, the head grower, says he liked to use bat guano, he learned it was destroying animal habitats and instead set out to find vegan and organic methods of meeting the plants' needs.

The biggest challenges facing Ganja Ma are mold and powdery mildew. It is constantly testing and researching new methods to keep the integrity of the process and quality high while preventing and eliminating mold and mildew.

The day before harvest, large sun leaves are stripped off the plants while they are still in the ground, leaving only the trichome-covered sugar leaves and buds on the stems. Plants are harvested in the dark shortly before sunrise. They are cut at the base with a pruning saw and hung upside down in a dark barn outfitted with fans and dehumidifiers if necessary. Although Ganja Ma tries to avoid harvesting in bad weather, it combats inevitable wet harvests by using a gentle leaf blower to remove mold-causing moisture from the buds' crevices. In dryer weather up to two weeks are required for a "nice slow dry."

Once the plants are sufficiently dry, the branches are cut down and wrapped inside cones of brown kraft paper. After a few more days drying in the paper, the branches are moved into plastic tubs that are burped a few times. They remain in the tubs in a cool, dark dry space until they are to be trimmed.

When it is time to cut the buds, the trim room is prepared with a deep cleaning and plastic sheets are laid on the floor. The trimming space receives good natural light that is supplemented with strong lamps at each trimmer's station. The trim bins are sterilized and pets are prohibited from the area. Trimmers are required to wear gloves while working to protect the product from contamination and the trimmers from intoxication.

Ganja Ma's advice to other growers? Be sure to grow with organic methods and in full sun to produce what is best for the body, spirit and the whole planet

9

Drying

PROPERLY GROWN, DRIED AND cured flowers burn smoothly and taste flavorful. The smell and flavor come from the terpenes and flavonoids in the buds. Terpenes also contribute to the strain's specific effects.

For buds to be proud of, think "low and slow." Drying and curing flowers takes time and patience, but the finished buds are worth the wait.

"Low" refers to temperature. Terpenes evaporate at different temperatures, and some at slightly below room temperature. When the air is fragrant with flower odors, the buds are losing their terpenes. Improperly dried and cured buds lose terpenes due to evaporation.

For example, the terpene myrcene—found in mango fruit, hops, bay leaves, eucalyptus, lemongrass and cannabis—evaporates at just 68º F (20º C). In addition to contributing to the smell, myrcene has analgesic, antibacterial, anti-inflammatory, anti-depressant and anti-anxiety properties and helps THC cross the blood/brain barrier. Terpenes are essential to cannabis consumers. Buds must be dried at low temperatures for the terpenes to be preserved. Drying at low temperatures and moderate humidity takes longer, hence "low and slow."

Keeping the area clean is imperative when slowly drying buds at low temperatures. Do not allow pets in the area because they shed fur and dander that become airborne and catch on sticky buds. Workers should wear gloves. Fungal spores and bacteria are ubiquitous and germinate under favorable conditions: moist environment, oxygen, temperatures between 50 and 70° F (10-21° C) and an acidic surface on the host.

Buds infected with powdery mildew are considered unfit for smoking but have not been implicated in any human ailments.

Buds attacked by bacteria turn brown and crispy. When anaerobic bacteria attack, they emit an acrid ammonia gas that turns buds to mush.

[Photo by David Downs @Rambling Rose Farms]

Under cool conditions the plant's cells stay alive for up to 72 hours after cutting. During the early part of drying, the plant consumes some of its store of water and carbohydrates. Dried too fast, the buds use fewer starches, resulting in a harsher smoke. Cells on the surface of the plant die first, and the ones farther inside die last. During the first stage of drying, water loss is rapid. At the same time some of the chlorophyll degrades, creating a smooth smoke. Buds dried slowly and then cured for a few weeks develop the smooth draw of fine herb. Rushed drying locks in chlorophyll leaving a "green," minty taste and a rougher smoke.

Degraded THC

Heat and light degrade THC into cannabinol (CBN), which has only a fraction of the psychotropic effect and induces sleepiness. When buds, especially large ones, are dried at high temperatures to speed the process, they dry unevenly. By the time the inner portion is dry, some of the THC on the outer portion has turned to CBN.

SMALL-SCALE DRYING

The drying needs of a small scale grower are the same as those of a large scale grower, but climate control is less of a challenge.

Climate-controlled drying box: Find a climate-controlled drying box such as a grow tent, large appliance box, or construct one using wood and plastic or plasterboard walls. Add a hygrometer connected to a small dehumidifier and a thermostat regulating a heater or air conditioner.

Drying in a bag: A brown paper bag is a simple way to keep humidity higher than the humidity in a room; this slows evaporation. Recirculate humidity by opening or closing the bag. To keep the humidity lower, place only two or three layers of big buds in the bag.

Use a hygrometer to measure the moisture level in the bag. If the humidity climbs above 50%, use a fan to remove moisture-laden air.

Closed, humidity-neutral space: A small room or a closet is likely to have the right temperature for drying. If not, adjust the conditions by opening or closing the door and using a fan. For more control, use a heater, air conditioner, humidifier, or dehumidifier as needed.

Rack drying: The advantage of rack drying is that air flows freely around the buds. Using fans to circulate the air shortens drying time.

Top Left & Right: These plants were about 4 1/2' tall with colas that stretch 15-18'. They are hung from a rod.

Bottom: The fan leaves are removed by hand. The buds are manicured after they dry and cure.

NOT A DRYING SPACE

Don't dry buds in a room with growing plants because the conditions required for the two operations are incompatible. The humidity and temperature in the growing room are likely to be too high for proper drying. The result may be mold attacks and loss of terpenes through evaporation.

Never dry in jars or closed containers

Buds should neither be dried nor cured in an enclosed container such as a closed box, plastic container or jar that traps air. As the buds dry, humidity in the container builds up and water is likely to condense on the sidewalls of the container, increasing the ambient moisture. These are ideal conditions for mildews, molds and bacteria to thrive.

Mold and mildew are likely to attack in closed containers, causing rot (botrytis) and molds. The fungi and aerobic bacteria use up the oxygen and anaerobic bacteria, which thrive in a non-oxygen environment. Their telltale sign is the acrid odor of ammonia they emit.

Molds, mildews and bacteria have a devastating effect on the terpenes and flavonoids (taste molecules); infected marijuana loses its distinctive odors and smells earthier.

None of the conditions created by closed containers are good for buds. The microorganisms can quickly turn a good harvest into waste.

The concept of using a closed container for either drying or curing is an urban myth. People often "burp" (open) the jars during drying to remove excess humidity. However, the humidity is trapped until the burping takes place, encouraging the proliferation of molds.

Steps to Drying

1. Clean the space to be used for drying. If it has been used for harvests before, wipe it clean with a hydrogen peroxide solution or just spray the whole space using it. This decreases microorganisms on surfaces. To keep air free from mold spores, hang a UVC sterilizing light and set up a carbon filter to cleanse the air of odor, particulates and microorganisms.

2. Use an air conditioner and a heater to maintain a temperature of about 68° F (20° C) in the drying area. Set the humidifier/dehumidifier to maintain humidity at 50%. When relative humidity is higher than 55%, the germination and growth of fungi and bacteria on wet material proliferates after about two or three days. Humidity be-

low 45% promotes faster drying, but at that humidity level big buds have a tendency to dry on the outside while the inside remains moist.

3. Turn on oscillating circulation fans to keep air moving throughout the space.

4. Add buds by hanging them or laying them on screens. Don't flat-dry flower buds or branches on screens if intending to machine trim them. Gravity compresses the part of the bud touching the surface. Trimming machines don't work well when fed flat-dried buds.

5. Monitor the buds during the drying process. This process can last from one to three weeks. Bud size, crop weight, crop moisture, ambient temperature and humidity all affect drying time.

6. Leave a dim light on throughout the drying process.

It is important to keep the air in the drying room flowing over the buds. The Vortex Powerfan is a sleek, silent fan perfect for the drying room. The speed-controlled and balanced motor with permanently lubricated ball bearings ensure long-term, vibration-free operation.

Keep the Equipment Clean

It is important to clean equipment in the drying room frequently because fungi and bacteria can colonize air conditioning units, humidifiers and dehumidifiers. Remove and clean the filter and spray the interior with a 3% hydrogen peroxide solution. Allow all parts to dry before reassembling.

WHEN DRYING IS COMPLETE

As the buds dry, they lose color and weight and become more brittle. The green color fades a bit as chlorophyll degrades, making yellow, brown, red and purple hues more prominent.

The first stage of drying is complete when buds feel dry on the outside but retain moisture inside that keeps them fairly pliable. Take an average-sized bud and slowly try to fold it in half. If the bud stem bends, the bud is still too wet. If the bud stem breaks, it's ready to be cured. If it breaks with a crisp snap, it is ready to cure. Another way of subjectively judging readiness is by lighting up a thinly rolled joint. If it doesn't go out between puffs, then it is ready for curing and storing.

Buds on cut whole plants take a longer time to dry than on cut branches and trimmed buds because there's more vegetation and thus more water to evaporate. But the slower cure mellows the taste. Big, thick, dense buds take much longer to dry than smaller buds and are more susceptible to mold and powdery mildew.

DRYING OUTDOORS

The main factors that affect outdoor drying are the same as indoors: temperature and humidity. However, dealing with these factors outdoors is more complicated because humidity and temperature vary over the course of a day. Starting in the morning at sunrise, the day begins to heat, drying any dew that set during the evening. Heat accumulates until midafternoon when the temperature drops, increasing relative humidity (RH) and the chance that dew will fall. Even in areas with small rises and drops, there may be danger during the hottest part of the day and then again as dew drips onto the plants.

Keep plants away from the sun's heating rays using white reflective material that bounces rather than absorbs the light.

In the shade: Provided the ambient temperature and humidity stay in a moderate range—50-68° F (10-20° C) temperature and 40-55% humidity—plants can be dried outdoors. The evening humidity and temperature are critical. Moisture from dew promotes infections. An area exposed to dew is unsuitable for drying unless a dehumidifier to eliminate the moisture. Another possibility is to maintain temperature at 68° using a heter, so there is no increase in RH.

In a covered area with no sidewalls: An outdoor area that is covered and has no sidewalls is suitable for drying, provided the temperature and humidity stay within range. Fans may be needed to remove dew and to cut down on midday heat and morning humidity.

Quick Drying, or Ways Not To Dry Buds

There are several methods to dry marijuana quickly for testing, but none will yield high-quality, well-dried, well-cured buds. However, fast-dried buds are an indication of what to expect once the rest of the harvest is dried. Fast-dried buds retain their minty chlorophyll taste and have a harsh smoke.

▶ Place the buds in the microwave for 30 seconds or longer so some of the moisture is removed and then lower the power to 2 and dry the buds until dry enough to test. Microwaves kill seeds, so buds containing desired seeds should not be microwaved.

▶ Food dehydrators fast-dry buds, but many of the terpenes evaporate in the elevated temperature. They never get very hot, so the THC remains but the flavors dissipate. This kills seeds.

▶ Place the small bud on top of a warm appliance such as a computer or refrigerator.

▶ Don't try drying marijuana in an oven unless it has a very low setting. Even so, the heat may evaporate the terpenes before the buds are dried. Set the temperature at 100° F (38° C) if possible. This may kill seeds.

Top: *Women strip buds from branches in Khandwa, Madya Pradesh, india, 1981*

Bottom: *The buds were spread out in the field about 8" deep to bake in the sun. Both aerobic and anaerobic decomposition took place due to the moisture and heat.*

Top: Pile of rejected material. In the rear, the nugs are spread out again for more drying.
Bottom: Choosing buds ready for packaging after four days of drying. They compressed into tight, brown, 1" long pieces. Inside they are fairly sticky. Now a worker is selecting buds, leaving behind seeds, dessicated leaves and small nugs.

Top: Worker in Rif mountains of Morocco stacks sheaths of single bud plants to dry.

Bottom: Unharvested fields will soon be cut. Meanwhile the harvested plants are drying. They will be placed in sheds until the winter and then turned into hash when the temperature dips below freezing. This facilitates processing by making the trichomes more brittle.

Whole plants drying in a barn in Switzerland in 2000, when it was legal.

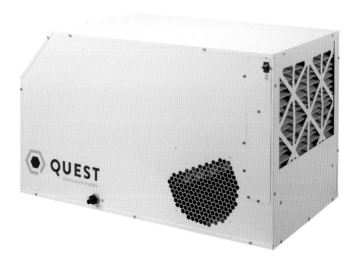

Cannabis killers including powdery mildew and bud rot can't take hold in your drying rooms if you properly control humidity. Dehumidifiers such as the Quest Dual 225 are designed specifically for the cannabis industry. The water pulled from the air is safe to reuse on subsequent grows.

REHYDRATING OVER-DRIED BUDS

There are plenty of myths and old-fashioned methods for rehydrating over-dried buds. One calls for placing fresh flour tortillas or fruit in a sealed container with the buds so they can absorb the moisture from them. Using fresh fruit to rehydrate buds is unsanitary.

Either put the buds in a climate-controlled room with increased humidity, about 70%, or use a teakettle to produce steam. Place the buds in a Rubbermaid container, add a little steam and close the lid tightly. Leave the steam in the container for a couple of hours. Check the buds to determine if they are remoistened enough or if they are too moist and need to be dried again.

Though worth trying, these methods cannot salvage buds that have lost their terpenes due to overdrying.

DETERMINING MOISTURE CONTENT OF MARIJUANA AND CONCENTRATES

The moisture percentage of marijuana is an important figure to know. The percentages when buds go from drying to curing to packaging for sale are, for the most part, mysterious and subjective. In this book we provide various tests to determine the stages of post-harvest processing. None of them are a true objective measurement though the community uses them all the time for want of a better system.

When I asked bud processors about this gap some had theories of what the proper moisture content should be, but few were even willing to venture a guess on quantifying a particular sample. Processors also had theories on the proper humidity (and temperature) of the drying, curing and storage areas and can dial that combination using automatic climate control.

One way to measure moisture percentage of leaf or bud is to weigh a small amount. Then place it in an oven at 80° F, until it is crispy dry and contains no moisture. Measure the difference and divide that number by the weight of the wet material. The resulting number is the percentage of moisture.

EXAMPLE:

A hundred grams of dried un-manicured buds were weighed out. Then they were placed in a low temp for 15 minutes maximum. When they were weighed again their weight came to 91.5 grams, a difference of 8.5 grams from their pre-treatment weight. 8.5 divided by the weight of the original, results in the percentage of moisture (8.5%) in the un-treated bud.

If there were an objective tool that can help with this chore, processors would have a more accurate assessment, taking the determination from the skill of an artisan to the eye of a trained worker.

There are at least two styles of moisture meters. One comes with two probes about 1-1½ inches apart sticking out less than half an inch. I think this is inconvenient. The kind I prefer has a touch pad sensor.

I get the most accurate results when I set the meter on the "softwood" setting and hold the material firmly against the pad with a piece of hard plastic. The readout takes about a second.

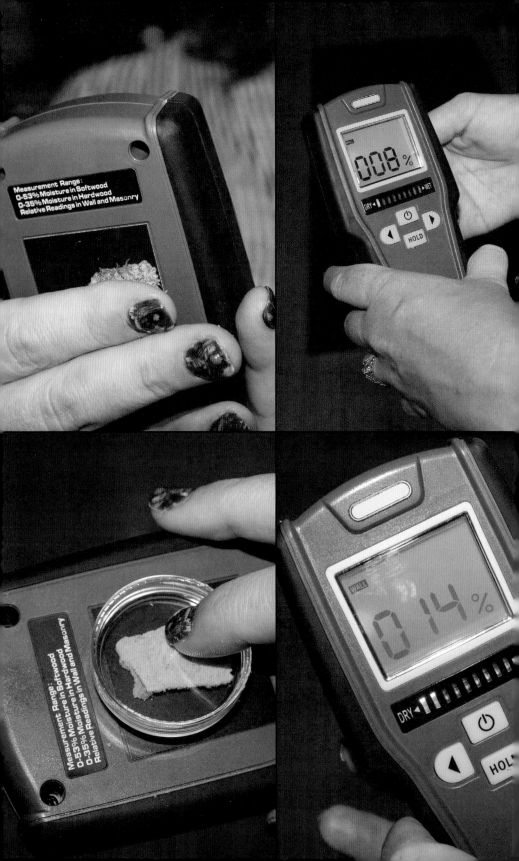

Even if the actual number isn't exactly accurate, if it's consistent, it can be used as a standard. In the cannabis community there has been a widespread opinion that 12% moisture is a good content of water for smoking in a joint that won't go out and is also the percentage at which small sticks snap. If you have tested the meter against these two subjective but accurate tests and the meter reads 12%, all is well. However, should the meter have a different readout, but it is consistent, you might not get the accurate percentage, but you will always know the bud is ready when it hits that number.

From my experiments and measurements I have some readouts and observations:

Proposed moisture readings for various humidity levels of processing and smoking:
Drying ends: 14-15%
Curing ends: 11-12%
Pleasant smoke: 10-12%
Harsh dry smoke: 10% or less

Note: Although these tests were performed with a meter designed for wood, other types of meters including hay and tobacco meters may also be used for testing. Experiment and find what works for you.

Top Left: A photo of the first trial of the moisture meter. We found that the moisture in the finger can affect the reading. (Photo model: Ellen Holland)

Top Right: The reverse side of the meter shows the readout.

Bottom Left: A piece of compressed kief. We used plastic, glass and metal plates to separate finger from the material. The readings seemed to be more accurate.

Bottom Right: Readout from the kief trial.

Garden Profile: Empress Extracts
Alameda County, California

MARKET: Medical
SIZE: 80 lights
LIGHTING: Indoor HPS
MEDIUM: Hydroponic, coconut coir and perlite
YIELD: Approximately 32 crops annually

Empress Extracts provides the San Francisco Bay Area with buds and dabbable hash oils. Crops are harvested every 12 to 15 days. The buds are immediately sorted into A and B nugs. The A buds are packaged and sold to dispensaries; the smaller buds are used to make fresh-frozen "nug-run" hash. Each plant produces about 0.25 pound (113 g) of buds, with about 60% A buds and 40% B buds for hashing.

They grow many strains including The Black, Boggle Gum, Chernobyl, Cookies/Jack the Ripper, Dosi Do, Duchess, Dutch Dragon, Empress OG (White OG), Mendo Breath, Sunset Sherbet, THC Bomb and White Goo.

Plants are forced to flower when they are about 2 feet (0.6 m) tall. They double in size during flowering, reaching 5 feet (1.5 m), easily filling the gardens at ripening. Strain choices are based on production quality, uniqueness and overall enjoyment of the finished product.

The plants' nutrient needs are met through synthetic liquid nutrients, foliar feeds, root drenches and full plant dips. Varieties are chosen based on quality and yield.

Tracking, planting, and scheduling allow Empress Extracts to create realistic harvest expectations. Toward the end of flowering, the buds are observed daily with a microscope to monitor terpene progression and determine the best day to pick.

Rooms are harvested all at once. Workers cut the plants at the base, deleaf them and hang them whole.

Then the branches are moved and hung to dry in a dark room set at about 70° F (21° C) and a relative humidity of 55%. Once the branches are dry enough to easily snap off buds, the dried buds are removed and placed in paper bags, which are rolled shut so the buds can cure. Once a day the bags are opened, rotated and resealed.

Plants are manicured once they are completely dry. Empress Extracts prefers to cut after the cure. Buds not destined for hashing are hand trimmed by one of three full-time trimmers. Trimmed buds are stored in turkey bags, which are opened for 30 minutes daily until they are sold.

The company's biggest challenge is keeping up with the day-to-day maintenance of the growing plants while constantly harvesting. Plants are checked individually and watered by hand; every plant gets detailed attention so its needs can be met immediately.

Empress Extract's advice to other growers? When harvesting, make sure the climate is temperate, dark and dry! Hanging branches too close together is an easy way to ruin amazing medicine because the buds are unable to dry properly and mold more easily.

Prevous page: Fresh cut whole plants in the dryroom.

Top Left: Green Man Cannabis Garden ready for harvest.

Top Right: Left: Plants are weighted.

Middle Right: Plants are tagged

10

Curing

THE FIRST PHASE OF drying is about removing the vast majority of water in the plant, which takes 1 to 3 weeks. The second phase, removing most of the remaining water while retaining the terpenes, is known as curing. It is analogous to the wine-aging process in that it uses a precise climate and time to bring out the aromas of the plant.

Curing is essential to the taste and experience of the finished buds. Like aged wines, well-cured buds are smooth and flavorful. Uncured buds still "work" but are not nearly as enjoyable or desirable. However, curing does not make buds more potent than they already are.

KEYS TO CURING

1. Start with mostly dried buds or colas. The bud stems may be just brittle enough to snap after bending a bit.

2. Set up a climate-controlled environment with consistent temperature and relative humidity so the buds lose water at a stable, slow pace.
   - Temperature: 65-70° F (18-21° C)
   - Humidity: 50-55%
   - Continuous circulation using oscillating and/or ceiling fans on low
   - Buds or colas placed loosely on trays, in boxes, or hung on lines.

Drying and curing in an open or partially closed bag is popular because it's convenient and it slows down the drying time of small batches so they don't dry out too rapidly.

3. Time: 10 to 30 days

4. Light: Constant dim light

TIME

The buds dry slowly and consistently over several weeks. Curing allows the terpenes, which are oils, to continue to evolve. The trichomes continue to dry and smooth out and the THC-acid (THCa) converts to Δ9-tetrahydrocannabinol (THC).

DARKNESS

Bright light, especially ultraviolet light, degrades cannabinoids and terpenes. Curing buds must sit in low light to total darkness.

Think Outside the Jar

Cannabis should not be cured in a sealed container. The water condenses on the inside, and bacteria and fungal spores thrive in the enclosed environment. Fungal spores and bacteria are ubiquitous and germinate under favorable conditions: moist environment, oxygen, temperatures between 50 and 70° F (10-21° C) and acidity.

Usually the first to attack are aerobic molds. They destroy terpenes and chlorophyll, changing the odor to earthy and the color from green to brown. When all the oxygen is used up, anaerobic bacteria start to grow. The acrid smell of ammonia is a telltale sign the bacteria are at work. They leave the buds crumbly.

Bud is suffering from Botrytis (Brown or Grey mold) as well as powdery mildew. These are the two molds most likely to attack cannabis.

OPTIMAL CURING SPACES

To maintain an optimal controlled curing climate, four simple, cheap appliances may be needed:

- Air conditioner (to cool and potentially dehumidify the room)
- Heater
- Humidifier (to add humidity and warmth)
- Dehumidifier (to dehumidify and add warmth)

Pros of Room Curing

DELICACY
Handle the material as minimally as possible. Each bud movement breaks off trichomes and decreasing value. By curing in a room the buds remain undisturbed.

LESS LABOR AND TIME
Batch curing a large, room-sized crop requires much less human labor and time, and hence cost, than curing in small containers such as jars or buckets.

DRYING STRAIGHT INTO STORAGE

Some growers don't mark a strict line between drying and curing. They leave the crop in place in a controlled drying room until it's time to bag for storage. The only time the buds are touched is during trimming for use or packaging.

Buds drying in cardboard boxes. The pile in each box is 2-3 inches deep. Opening and closing the lids is used to regulate the drying rate.

WATER CURING

Water curing cannabis has been gaining traction with growers. Considering one of the biggest challenges to properly harvesting and curing buds is maintaining proper climate to prevent the growth of mold, soaking the freshly harvested buds in water may seem counterintuitive. It's not.

Water curing removes excess salts from improperly flushed buds, and while it isn't always the best cosmetic choice, it creates finished buds with a smooth smoke and good flavor.

Traditional curing, or air curing, cannot remove excess salts that are not purged during the flush. Traditional air curing is the best method for buds that are destined to be sold on store shelves because there is no cosmetic disruption.

Water cured buds, though less aesthetically pleasing, are incredibly smooth. Additionally, growers planning to water cure their buds can skip the flush and encourage more vigorous growth while the plant is ripening. Planning to water cure and skipping the flush could increase the yield.

HOW TO WATER CURE

Cut harvested branches so they fit in the container they will be cured in. Remove the fan leaves. A hydrogen peroxide and water bath should be used before the water cure begins to remove fungal and mold spores, dirt and debris that become stuck to the gooey buds.

Use only low PPM water. Water from the tap may contain the excess salts and minerals the grower is trying to flush out of the plant.

Submerge freshly washed buds in the water, using a heavy item to weigh them down and prevent floating without smashing the buds.

Water should be maintained at room temperature, about 65-75° F (18-24° C). In cold water, trichomes will snap off when agitated.

Change the water daily and keep the buds submerged for 1-4 days.

Some of the contents held in the leaves and buds are water-soluble and will dissolve during this process. These include fertilizer salts, chlorophyll, and some dirt and debris.

Long-term water curing (right bud) reduced the yield and potency of the bud. The bud on the left is air cured. [Photo by Sidney Borghino]

Cannabinoid Profiling

WET CURE

Analysis of major cannabinoids by advanced chromatography. [GC: SOP-010; HPLC: SOP-014]

	GC		HPLC	
	Percent	mg/g	Percent	mg/g
d9-THC	NA	NA	2.44	24.44
d8-THC	NA	NA	0.00	0.00
THCA	NA	NA	12.62	126.25
THCV	NA	NA	0.01	0.11
CBC	NA	NA	0.05	0.45
CBG	NA	NA	0.04	0.45
CBGA	NA	NA	0.04	0.42
CBN	NA	NA	0.04	0.39
CBD	NA	NA	0.02	0.16
CBDV	NA	NA	0.03	0.35
CBDA	NA	NA	0.04	0.42
Total	NA	NA	15.34%	153.43

~16% Decarboxylated THC

Microbiological Screening

Petriflim screening for microbiological contamination. [SOP-009]

	Count	Limit	Status
APC	TNTC*	100,000	Fail
Yeast & Mold	0	10,000	Pass
Coliform	TNTC*	100	Fail
E coli	0	10	Pass
Pseudomonas	0	0	Pass
Salmonella	0	0	Pass

Cannabinoid Profiling

DRY CURE

Analysis of major cannabinoids by advanced chromatography. [GC: SOP-010; HPLC: SOP-014]

	GC		HPLC	
	Percent	mg/g	Percent	mg/g
d9-THC	NA	NA	0.90	8.95
d8-THC	NA	NA	0.00	0.00
THCA	NA	NA	18.84	188.36
THCV	NA	NA	0.00	0.04
CBC	NA	NA	0.03	0.33
CBG	NA	NA	0.07	0.75
CBGA	NA	NA	0.13	1.33
CBN	NA	NA	0.03	0.29
CBD	NA	NA	0.00	0.00
CBDV	NA	NA	0.04	0.39
CBDA	NA	NA	0.05	0.48
Total	NA	NA	20.09 %	200.93

~5% Decarboxylated THC

Microbiological Screening

Petriflim screening for microbiological contamination. [SOP-009]

	Count	Limit	Status
APC	50,000	100,000	Pass
Yeast & Mold	5,000	10,000	Pass
Coliform	0	100	Pass
E coli	0	10	Pass
Pseudomonas	0	0	Pass
Salmonella	0	0	Pass

If the water is not changed daily it becomes cloudy. This should be avoided because the water can become a microbial soup. One way to prevent this is to use a 1% solution of hydrogen peroxide (one part drug store 3% hydrogen peroxide to two parts water).

Once the cure is done, hang the buds to dry as usual.

In a single controlled experiment testing similar buds from the same plant, one air dried and one water cured, the water cured bud tested significantly lower in THC-a/THC, a total of about 5% less.

Notice the failure for yeast and E Coli in the water cured bud (top document). If hydrogen peroxide was used in the wash this probably would not have happened. Testing courtesy Steep Hill Labs.

Right: The spoon kept the bud submerged. [Photo by Sidney Borghino]

WATER CURING FOR EDIBLES

Water curing is an excellent method to cure buds destined for consumption in infused foods, or edibles, because the process removes chlorophyll, which causes the "green taste" people dislike in food infusions. A soak as short as one day will remove most of the chlorophyll and significantly change the taste. The flavor of butters or oils infused with water-cured buds is often more pleasing to many consumers.

IMPROVING POORLY CURED BUDS

As mentioned earlier, buds can be cleaned using a 1% hydrogen peroxide water bath. This removes much of the chlorophyll. They should soak for a day or less.

Patients with compromised immune systems should consider a hydrogen peroxide water cure to assure medicine is clean, safe and contains no mold or fungal spores.

Small-Scale Curing

1. Use a climate-controlled space that can be maintained at 50% humidity and a temperature of 70° F (21° C) to age the buds during curing.

2. If the buds have been manicured after initial drying, place them on screen trays. If they haven't been touched, leave the plants, branches or colas in trays or hanging.

3. Leave buds alone in the dark. The more they are handled, especially if they are naked, the more cannabinoid- and terpene-filled glands are lost.

4. Maintain a consistent climate for 10 days or longer.

5. Test the buds. Fully cured buds are ready when the stems of thick buds break with a clean snap, but the bud is still pliable. It should support burning in a joint.

METHODS

Many home cultivators lack a room they can climate control. The following are alternatives:

Paper Bags

A heated area probably has low humidity. If the space has low humidity (less than 45% RH), keep the buds from getting too dry by wrapping them individually in newspaper. Tape the paper shut, but do not seal the ends. Leave the packages loosely packed so they can breathe and place in a cool, dark room. The semi-permeable paper enclosure maintains a higher relative humidity than the room it is in.

Jars and Containers

Despite being popular, sealed container curing is not recommended. This method requires more work and there is a high possibility the crop will be destroyed.

Growers planning on using jars or any other closed containers to cure must make sure they are consistently available to check on and attend to the containers.

To cure in jars, start by preparing a cool, dark space with a stable climate.

1. Clean the curing prep table and instruments. Transport trimmed buds to the table.

2. Fill each jar 2-8 inches (5-20 cm) deep with buds, but not more than half full. Do not overfill, pack or tamp the buds in any way. If the buds are slightly moist, fill only a few inches. With drier buds the container can be filled deeper.

3. Separate buds by size. Big buds retain water longer than smaller ones making uniform drying difficult, so dry them separately. Another solution is to break up the big buds.

Cover the jars loosely to start. Let the containers sit for two to four hours and then check them. If the buds have started "sweating," or creating condensation on the inside of the jar, they are too wet and need to dry more. Either remove them from the jar, or more perilously, just remove the cover.

Sweating indicates a high humidity and condensation, not only on the container's interior, but also on the buds. Invariably, with even mild sweating, aerobic bacteria become active and can change the aroma and taste. Some people enjoy that mild ferment, but it indicates the destruction of chlorophyll and terpenes. Further, in this environment bacteria proliferate. Jar-cured marijuana rarely passes dispensary tests for bacteria.

If there is even the slightest sweating, return the buds to the drying area. If the buds cannot be moved, burp the jars: Open them to remove the humidity. Let fresh air in for four to five minutes, and then replace the lids. During the first day this may need to be done every hour or two. Letting the jars sit overnight without burping can spell disaster. Leaving the lids off the jars prevents problems.

1. Days 2-7: When burping, gently roll containers to reposition the buds inside; rough handling damages resin glands, so be gentle. Smell the expelled air during burping. At first it will smell damp and vegetative. Burp the buds frequently. Don't wait for telltale odors indicating mold (earthy vegetative) or bacteria (ammonia). If an odor is detected, return the buds to the drying room.

2. Day 7: Reduce burping to once a day unless there are any telltale odors. If there are, increase the burping rate.

3. Day 14: Reduce burping to 2-4 times per week.

4. Day 21: The buds should be ready, but curing can last much longer. Chlorophyll odors should be gone. Terpenes should be at their peak prominence. A bud's pigments are expressed more without chlorophyll's green dominance. When pinched, a nug should be dry to the touch from the surface to the stem, but should bounce back from squeezing much like a sponge.

USING MOISTURE SENSORS TO REGULATE BURPING

Handheld moisture meters provide accurate humidity readings inside spaces and containers. There are both probe models and near-infrared readers. Dry the buds as normal and place them in jars. When the sensor says the relative humidity inside the jar is at 65%, burp the jar immediately. Over time, as the buds dry, the humidity will rise more slowly and the maximum humidity will fall. Once the humidity stops climbing above 55%, the bud has finished curing.

Miron glass bottle eliminates most light from passing through. This top measures the relative humidity.

USING MOISTURE PACKS

Returning moisture to over-dried buds with a moisture packet will not improve a cure. However, moisture packs can be used to rehydrate buds that will soon be consumed.

Bovida pack

Each Boveda pack consists of a specially prepared saturated solution of pure water and natural salt. This saturated solution is contained within a water-vapor permeable membrane. Within a closed desktop humidor Boveda maintains a predetermined level of RH by releasing or absorbing purified water-vapor, as needed, through the membrane.

Curing Myths: Don't Bury Buds

A long-running rumor involves burying buds to encourage certain microbes to eat them and secrete a more euphoric chemical. That's total nonsense. Do not smoke buds with any kind of mold on them. There is no way to boost potency after the plant is cut.

ASK ED:
Why Do People Cure in Sealed Containers If It Isn't Ideal?

Why is jar and bucket curing so prevalent if room curing is optimal?

Jar and bucket curing is popular because of habit and ritual. When growers find a process that works, near-religious rituals start to develop.

In the 20th century, cannabis prohibition prevented the creation of dedicated, climate-controlled curing rooms. Personal growers trying to avoid detection couldn't turn their homes into curing rooms. After cannabis was dry enough not to rot, growers had it jarred and stored offsite. Burping became a tedious necessity. It hurts hands, wrists and forearms and requires lots of regularly scheduled repetitive labor.

It just doesn't make sense. Jars are for sealing and storage. Sealing wet buds is a no-no. Why place buds in sealed jars if they need to be burped?

Now the industry is trending toward dedicated curing spaces. With legalization, inefficient techniques like burping, developed to overcome the challenges associated with cannabis prohibition, are becoming outdated in favor of legal environments where operations can effectively scale.

TIPS FOR THE ULTIMATE CURING ROOM

An ideal curing space should have the following:

- Water-resistant walls
- Air conditioner, heater, humidifier, dehumidifier and fans all on controllers
- Rolling racks of steel-mesh trays for buds or lines for hanging

---

ASK ED:
Curing for Hash?

Are there advantages in curing pot if it will be used to make extracts?
–Jeffrey S., Facebook

No. Depending on the process the plants may have to be dried, but in some processes even drying isn't required. If there is no heat in the process that is being used, the THC may remain in its inactive form.

TROUBLESHOOTING

Fast Curing

Sometimes there isn't enough time to cure and that's okay. Plenty of consumers can't tell the difference. There is no such thing as "fast curing": that's an oxymoron. By its nature, curing is a slow process that takes time.

Supply Chain Curing

The cannabis supply chain can act as a curing agent. A proper dry/cure takes about 20 days. Most of the time buds stay in the supply line for another 10 to 15 days before the client receives them. They continue to cure during that time. Factor on that extra curing time when planning your harvest.

Whole plant curing [Photo by David Downs @Ganja Ma Garden]

11

Storing

MARIJUANA QUALITY AND POTENCY change over time. In the living plant, the precursors of THC and CBD are found in their acid forms, THCa and CBDa. These are not psychotropic. Only when they lose a portion of their molecules do they become active as THC and CBD. This occurs naturally over time and is accelerated in the presence of heat and light, especially ultraviolet light.

Once buds are dried and cured, potency is at its peak. Over time THC gradually degrades to CBN, a far less psychotropic cannabinoid than THC.

Research conducted at the University of Mississippi on low-quality cannabis stored for four years at room temperature (68-72° [20-22° C]) found that the percentage loss of THC was proportional to time in storage, with the greatest loss in the first year. As the THC level declines, the concentration of CBN increases.

YEARS IN STORAGE	TOTAL THC LOSS	ANNUAL NET THC LOSS
1	16.6%	-
2	26.8%	10.2%
3	34.5%	7.7%
4	41.4%	6.9%

This research is consistent with the experiences of marijuana users. Marijuana loses potency over time as the psychoactive THC converts to CBN, which induces sleep but not highness. Storing buds in the freezer or refrigerator slows deterioration. Freezing keeps buds fresh longest. However, even in deep freeze THC deteriorates, at nearly 4% a year. In deep freeze (below 0°F) deterioration slows further. At refrigerator temperatures THC deteriorates at

Tubs of trimmed buds [Photo by Darcy Thompson @North Bay Cultivators]

the rate of about 5.4% a year. A freezer is best for long-term storage; a refrigerator is good for protecting terpenes in the short term.

There are several problems with storing marijuana in a freezer, especially when supercooled to 0° F (-18° C):

Even under higher temperatures in the freezer, glands become very brittle and are easily and inadvertently shaken off buds. For that reason, once placed in the freezer the container should be handled very gently and when removed the buds should be given time to warm up so they become more pliable.

The moisture in the container freezes and can form ice crystals, especially during long storage. This may also occur when buds have not been dried sufficiently.

However, in several experiments, properly dried marijuana in a plastic container developed no ice crystals when placed in a freezer for several months. The trichomes remained intact. If moisture is a problem, vacuum sealing mostly eliminates it, although the process may result in crushed buds. Another solution is to remove the air with moisture-free gas such as carbon dioxide or nitrogen. These can be injected into the container as the ambient air exits through another hole. Then both holes are sealed.

When freezing marijuana in glass containers, choose shoulderless containers as shouldered containers are more likely to develop cracks. Metal and wood containers can also be used for freezing.

One way to store frozen marijuana is in small containers. Pack just enough for a week's use in each container. The rest of the stored material is not disturbed so the glands are not at risk., as they can be removed from the freezer individually.

According to the University of Mississippi study, refrigerator temperatures slow deterioration to alittle less than 0.5% a month, which isn't noticeable when storing for just a few months. Here, too, it is best if the bulk of the stored material is disturbed infrequently.

Heat and light, especially UV light, evaporate terpenes and erode quality. Only an opaque container will completely protect the terpenes and therefore the quality of the buds stored inside. An opaque container with a white exterior reflects heat, keeping the contents cool. Using a desiccant packet that maintains a set humidity of about 60-65% ensures the proper level of moisture is retained without causing mold.

Terpene molecules vary in size, and the smallest ones evaporate at lower temperatures, starting in the high 60s. Buds kept at room temperature in an open container will experience some loss of terpenes. Storing buds in a refrigerator or freezer keeps terpenes in a liquid state, rather than gassing off.

> ## Storage Moisture
>
> **Dried buds should be stored in a space or container that maintains a humidity level, ideally, around 60%, or within a range of 58-65%.**

STORING MATERIALS

Cannabis can be properly stored in a number of different materials, each with pros and cons that make them more or less suitable depending on the grower's needs.

Glass

Glass makes great, inert, hard, non-biodegradable storage containers. The downside is that most glass jars are clear, and light degrades trichomes—which doesn't matter if buds are stored in the dark. For storing buds exposed to light, an opaque glass is best.

Different types of glass are used to store food. The color of the glass determines the type of light and heat that can penetrate the barrier.

Top shelf bud stored in glass jars [Photo by Darcy Thompson @Harborside Health Center]

Violet Glass

Violet glass blocks visible light with the exception of the color violet. It also is semi-permeable to UV-A, an infrared light, allowing about 40-60% to penetrate, depending on glass formula and thickness.

Miron Glass, a manufacturer in Germany, claims that this combination of light preserves biological material such as herbs as well as fresh vegetation. They base their claims loosely on bio-photons, which is very weak light emitted by all living things. Their literature claims that even when material is dry, the light that penetrates the glass preserves this energy while forming a barrier to other visible spectrums that can cause deterioration of cannabinoids and terpenes.

Placing a glass or stainless steel container in a dark space such as a refrigerator closet or dark room will also keep harmful light out. It is highly unlikely that there is much UVA light indoors, so none is passing through. However, visible light is filtered out.

In a controlled experiment, fresh garden tomatoes were placed in a Miron container, a stainless steel container and a clear glass container. All were sealed and the clear glass container was kept entirely in the dark.

MyPharmJar is a violet glass storage system designed to keep dried herbs and buds fresh and prevent decay for years. The jars include a built-in humidity and temperature sensor to prevent mold and over-drying. The Miron glass prevents most light from penetrating the bottle, protecting quality and potency.

Stainless steel CVaults are the choice of many connoisseur growers, retailers and consumers. They're airtight, lightweight, nonporous, durable and impenetrable to light—the ultimate for storing buds. The bottoms are dishwasher safe, making them easy to clean. Sizes range from the X-Small Personal CVault Curing Storage Container to the 4.4-gallon (17 l) Mega CVault, which holds up to 2 pounds (1 kg) of dried buds.] [Photo by Darcy Thompson]

When the jars were opened a month later, the tomatoes were still fresh, if a little dehydrated. The containers were closed again and reopened a month later. All three tomatoes had begun molding at similar rates.

Stainless Steel

Stainless steel tubs with plastic seals and flip-top locking mechanisms are popular because they're strong and can be stacked. The metal does not interact with the buds and is impervious to outside air. Stainless steel containers are an excellent choice for storage.

Plastic

Cannabis is slightly acidic and lipophilic so it degrades some plastics. Plastics are stickier than glass or stainless steel. Odorless turkey bags are popular because they contain odors and are inexpensive. However, they are easily pierced by stems and offer no protection from shaking and movement, which leads to more damage and shake. Five-gallon buckets sealed with toothed, locking, airtight lids will protect buds from getting crushed and can be stacked.

Desiccants

A desiccant is a substance that removes moisture from the surrounding air. Desiccants are often found in certain food packages, like dried seaweed, and in electronics. Silicon packets, newspaper or anything extra-dry acts as a desiccant and absorbs moisture in a storage container.

For buds destined to be consumed soon, one space-saving solution is to use vacuum-sealed, food-grade Mylar pouches. To keep buds fresh longer, use nitrogen-flushed, sealed medical-grade pouches. [Photo by David Downs @ Bolder Cannabis]

True Liberty Bags are resistant to cold, heat, grease, oil and water The bags have an excellent aroma barrier that makes for a versatile container.

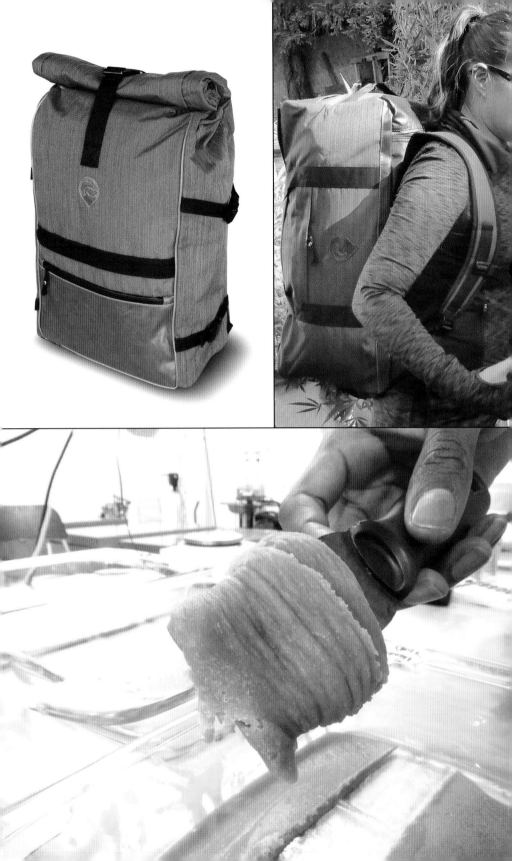

VACUUM SEALING

Vacuum packaging is popular because it decreases the amount of oxygen present in a storage container. Oxygen is corrosive and degrades the buds' color. Decreased presence of oxygen also discourages the growth of spoilage bacteria, but not anaerobic bacteria. Anaerobic bacteria thrive in low and no-oxygen environments that are damp and have food—the buds! Never seal and store wet or damp buds.

GAS-BASED STORING

Gas-flushed, sealed Mylar bags are excellent packaging for long-term storage. The process flushes the bag with nitrogen and seals it. Unlike oxygen, nitrogen is inert and doesn't burn. Purging packages of oxygen extends the life of the buds and prevents growth of mold and discoloration, similar to vacuum sealing. Some testing labs offer nitrogen bagging services using tamper-proof packaging.

STORING FRESH-FROZEN

Marijuana can be made directly into concentrates or stored undried and "wet" frozen to be used later. This saves of energy and labor. With storage, converting the material can be postponed to a more convenient time. Either fresh or frozen buds can be used for bubble, or BHO. First, the chopped buds are brought to near freezing temperature. Then agitation from a paint mixer or other tool makes the glands brittle; they break off and are collected in a series of filters that catch different sized glands. When collected, the glands can be used as an intermediate for making butane or CO_2 concentrate. BHO extractors use butane as a solvent to de-cannabinize and de-terpenize the leaf. The result is a very pure dabbable concentrate.

Storing Shatter

Extracts have narrower temperature tolerances. Shatter-type extracts start buddering (clouding over, which decreases value) at a little over 65° F (18° C). Prevent bubble hash from molding by sealing and storing it in a refrigerator or freezer.

Top: This roll up backpack by SkunkGuard uses activated-carbon technology to trap and neutralize odors and harmful chemicals. It is weatherproof and has adjustable straps to accommodate both large and small loads.

Bottom: Scrape of sugary wax extract [Photo by David Downs]

12

After The Harvest

AFTER THE HARVEST IS complete, growers are left with a variety of byproducts. What used to be considered trash is now processed further and enjoyed or sold. The first step is to evaluate and separate the material. The most efficient way is to sort it during trimming.

The quality of the remaining material is based on the percentage of THC and other cannabinoids it contains. Three types of growth remain after the buds have been removed: popcorn buds (larf), sugar trim and fan leaves. Stems and woody parts of the plant are not suitable for ingestion since they contain few cannabinoids.

GRADES OF TRIM

Popcorn Buds (Larf)

Buds that receive less light grow smaller and less dense. They are time consuming to trim and cosmetically undesirable in the market. However, they contain a high percentage of THC and are often used to make pre-rolls or concentrates.

Sugar Trim

Sugar trim refers to the resin-covered leaves that grow near and often sur-round the buds. They are cut during manicuring and other than the buds, contain the most THC in the plant. Sugar trim is used to make extracts such as kief, hash, tinctures and edibles.

Fan Leaves (Sun Leaves)

Although fan leaves contain a third or less of the cannabinoids as sugar trim, processing them may still be worthwhile. Leaves with visible glands are worth keeping. Leaves from immature plants typically have very few glands and do not yield much THC.

Use a magnifying glass or photographer's loupe for a closeup look at the material. Fan leaf glands are often small and hug the surface of the leaf, while glands near the flowers are stalked and look like mushrooms with bulbous caps. The latter contain considerably more cannabinoids than the smaller glands.

Male plants also contain cannabinoids. These cannabinoids are strongest at the budding, pre-flowering stage. The sugar leaves — small leaves near the flowers—are the most potent, followed by the younger and then the older fan leaves. Male plants are not prized for resin production and are often removed from the garden and destroyed.

- To use fan leaves in cooking, gently heat them in butter or oil. Use the infused oil in salads or cooking.
- Grind dried fan leaves into fine flour and substitute it for a small portion of regular flour in recipes. To remove the chlorophyll taste, soak the leaves in cool water before drying and grinding. The flour can also be used in making salves and poultices; an easy method is to mix it into an existing topical ointment.
- Juice the fresh leaves. Start by rinsing them and then run them through a wheatgrass juicer. To store for later, pour the juice into ice cube trays and freeze it. The juice is ingested medically and for general health maintenance.

Stems and branches contain little to no usable THC. However, there are several ways to recycle them:

- Chop and use as mulch.
- Use as fire kindling.
- Carve the large stems.
- Use as walking sticks
- Use for craft projects such as papermaking.
- Chop finely for superior horse bedding or small animal litter.

There are various ways to use the separated trim and maximize crop value. Trim, sugar leaves and popcorn buds can be converted to kief, hash, BHO, tinctures and cooking oils. For the purposes of this book, only safe, at-home extractions are covered. For more in-depth instructions and information on all post-harvest extractions, see our book Beyond Buds: Marijuana Extracts—Hash, Vaping, Edibles & Medicine.

KIEF

When the trichomes are separated from the plant material, they form a pale blonde to green powder known as kief. High-quality golden kief is consumed. Lower-quality green kief, which contains a lot of vegetation, is used for cooking or for further processing.

The blonde glands are delicious smoked fresh and loose and have a lighter, distinctively different flavor than the whole bud. They have not been heated, so the kief has a high concentration of terpenes. Some traditionalists insist that kief is best pressed into hash. It can also be sprinkled over a bowl or joint, or mixed in food. The simplest and most common method of making kief from sugar leaves or popcorn buds is by screening it.

Sifting kief

Screening for Kief

Use a fine screen. The size of the openings in the screen determines what size glands and how much residual plant material passes through. The vigor used in rubbing the plant material over the screen has a profound effect on the quality of the final product. Rub gently. More debris is pushed through when the screening is vigorous. Also, sifting the same material a few times yields more kief, but each sift results in a higher proportion of plant mixed with the glands.

Kief or pollen-sifting boxes and screens are good tools for processing small personal-use amounts. They can be as simple as wooden stash boxes with a screen above a pullout drawer to catch the glands that fall off buds from normal handling. Other boxes are made specifically to capture different grades. Use cold buds and trim because cold causes the trichomes to become brittle and break more easily.

Automatic kief makers called Pollinators and pollen sifters use tumbling action to rub leaves against a screen that separates the glands from the leaves. The rubbings are collected on a bottom plate.

Divide kief processing by time. The highest grade comes from the first minute of rubbing. The material degrades with each processing as the ratio of vegetation to glands increases.

HOW WATER HASH WORKS

The most common water hash processing method uses a combination of water, ice and agitation to separate glands from the plant material. Ice, water and plant material are placed in a bucket that has been lined with filtration bags with screens on the bottom similar to the screens used for making kief. The material is agitated to knock the trichomes free. Plant material is trapped and floats in the top bag while the glands, which are heavy, sink to the bottom and are collected in the bags.

Ready-made systems use multiple bags, usually 3-7 bags with various size screens to sort the glands into grades. Unlike kief making, the material is separated in one step rather than through repeated sieving. Usually the material is processed once, although some commercial hash makers process it a second time to capture more of the THC.

Kief color ranges from golden white for the purest kief to a greenish gold. The greener it is, the more plant material it contains. Only golden kief is enjoyable inhaled. The coarser greener material is used in cooking or for making topicals and concentrates.

Ice serves a dual purpose: It acts as an agitator against which the plant material rubs, and it makes the material very cold so the glands become brittle. After the material is agitated in ice water, it is allowed to settle. Then the bags are separated, and the glands are removed from each one. They vary in content. Different sized glands have different effects. After water hash is dried, it is ready to smoke.

Water hash varies in color, much like kief. The finest grade is typically a light tan, while the coarser second-tier material is slightly darker and may be a little green from plant material contamination.

Water hash can be made without bags. Agitate the material in ice and water for 20 minutes. A paint mixer attached to a motor or drill works well. After agitating, most of the plant material floats. Remove it using a colander and cooking spoon. Glands are heavier than water and detach from the vegetation. They sink to the bottom of the container where they form a gray or tan layer. Rinse them from the container and capture them in a coffee filter.

The quality of water hash, especially from the finest grade material, is impressive. It can test as high as many solvent-extracted hash products: up to 80%, although 50% samples are more common. The effects produced by water hash depend on the strain and quality of the plants. Processing plant material with water yields hash that has been washed free of some contaminants: green

Commercial farmers and hobby growers should consider True Liberty Bags to keep their buds fresh and potent. They are available in 3-quart, 2-gallon, 3-gallon, 5-gallon, 30-gallon, 55-gallon and "bottomless" sizes ranging from 12' x 20' to 24' x 500'.

plant matter, dust, dander and some mold, bacteria and chemicals. However, high counts of mold and bacteria are commonly found in tests of water hashes. Perhaps a final rinse in 1% Hydrogen Peroxide water will lower these counts.

Extraction yields 0.5 to 2 ounces (14-57 g) of hash per pound of plant material, depending on gland density and size.

MAKING BHO; BUDDER, SHATTER AND WAX

The popularity of products made using butane—hash oil, wax, budder and shatter—is surging for a number of reasons. These include strength, versatility in vape pens, and potential as purer, healthier ways to inhale THC and other cannabinoids. The THC content is often more than 80%. Butane hash oil (BHO) contains no vegetative material and few tars or other carcinogens. The extraction process kills bacteria and molds and other fungi present in the source material, but some toxins remain.

Processors prefer butane because it's inexpensive, easy to obtain and has good extraction efficiency. Also, the equipment is relatively inexpensive.

These techniques use butane to dissolve marijuana's active ingredients, cannabinoids and terpenes, from the plant matter. The solvent is then evap-

The "T-Rex," is designed for cannabis extraction without solvents at home. Simply place the buds in parchment paper, press for 10 seconds and the rosin is ready!

orated, leaving the resin, which can be refined into other products.

Butane extraction is by far the most popular chemical extraction method for marijuana because it's the cheapest technique available. Inexpensive equipment can be used to refine low-grade trim—although *this book* adamantly advises against it. Butane extraction is an industrial process best suited to professionals.

THE DANGER OF BHO

Butane is one of the most dangerous substances for making hash because it is very explosive. It is not recommended for home amateur extraction. At room temperature, butane is a flammable gas that's heavier than air. Instead of off-gassing and diffusing, it pools on the floor and flows until it dissipates. If it comes in contact with an open flame, such as a pilot light or hot water heater, just a spark of static electricity, or a lit joint or lighter, it explodes.

Because butane is heavier than air, it can pool on the ground in an area where it is being "open blasted." Open blasting is a dangerous way to make solvent hash oils at home because the butane is not being processed in a system that contains it. Any spark, or even a cell phone, can trigger an explosion in the place the oil is being extracted.

BHOgart extractors are closed-loop, meaning they capture and retain dangerous gasses that could cause explosions. Although solvent extraction is not recommended for home processing, BHO and other extracts are made safely using commercial closed-loop systems. Closed-loop systems are the safest and most efficient way to make these types of extractions in a professional setting. They are made with stainless steel, so they are easy to clean and keep sanitary.

DECARBOXYLATION

For raw cannabis to become psychotropic it must be decarboxylated. This converts the inactive forms, THCa and CBDa, to the active forms, THC and CBD. Heating raw buds during the smoking process ensures that decarboxylation takes place.

If BHO is to be used in edibles, it needs to be decarboxylated to make it psychotropic. This occurs over time, but the process speeds up exponentially with heat. THCa and CBDa decarboxylate into THC and CBD beginning at 222° F (106° C). BHO or buds that are going to be smoked or vaped do not need to be decarboxylated. The lighter or nail will take care of that instantly.

The problem is that the same temperature that turns THCa into THC

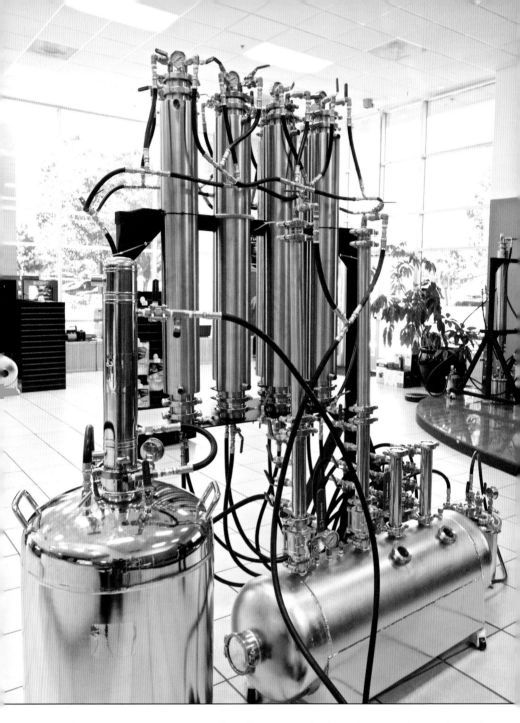

also turns THC into cannabinol (CBN), which is less psychotropic and more sedative than THC. When THCa is 70% decarboxylated into THC, the rate of THC-to-CBN production eclipses the rate of decarboxylation from THCa to THC.

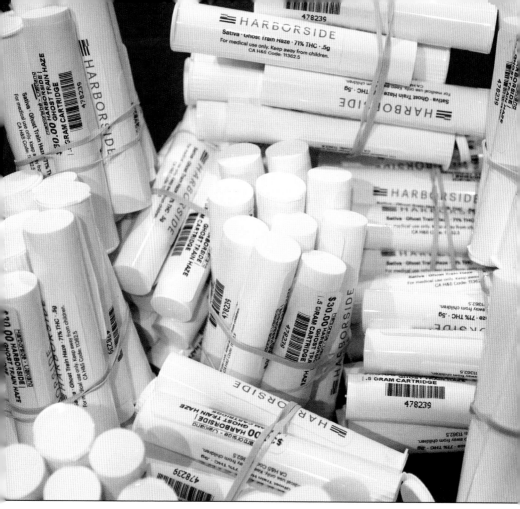

Vape Pen Cartridges [Photo by Darcy Thompson @Harborside Health Center]

TINCTURES

Before cannabis prohibition, tinctures were the most common way of buying and consuming marijuana in America. Recently, they've been making a comeback and are available in dispensaries in many states. Tinctures are discreet to use and quite easy to make at home.

A tincture is a concentrated extract of any herb in liquid—usually alcohol, sometimes glycerin—that is taken orally as a drop on or under the tongue. Alcohol is used to separate the cannabinoids, terpenes and other essential oils from the plant material and acts as a preservative. In herbal medicine, tinctures are commonly 25% alcohol, which is achieved by diluting the mixture with water. People who do not want to consume alcohol may opt for glycerin-based tinctures.

Methods of making alcohol tinctures of marijuana vary from extremely simple and low tech to complex distillation apparatuses that produce highly purified cannabis oil. The easiest way to make tinctures is an alcohol soak. All that's required is drinking alcohol of 80 proof or higher and cannabis leaves, trim, buds or kief. Add the cannabis to the liquor, let it soak for at least a week, then strain (or not) and enjoy. To make a tincture with less taste, soak the ground buds in tepid water for a day. Pour out the water, which contains strong-tasting, non-medical water solubles. Place an ounce of cannabis leaf in about a pint of alcohol. Figure that an ounce (28 g) of trim makes between 20 and 40 servings. No matter what type of cannabis is going into the tincture, starting with a quality solvent is important. The purist grade alcohol is USP medical-grade 190- or 200-proof neutral grain spirits. It is available from laboratory supply companies.

Tinctures [Photo by Darcy Thompson @Harborside Health Center]

More commonly available is 190-proof Everclear alcohol, which can be found at liquor stores in 40 of the 50 states. Note that Everclear is marketed in two strengths: 150 proof (75% alcohol) and 190 proof (95% alcohol). Get the 190 if possible. Sale of Everclear 190 is banned in California, Florida, Hawaii, Iowa, Maine, Minnesota, Nevada, New York, Ohio and Washington.

An alternative high-proof option available in some of those states and online is an extremely pure form of Polish vodka called Spirytus that is 192-proof (96% alcohol, or 1% purer than Everclear). Polmos Spirytus, Spirytus Rektyfikowany, and Baks Spirytus are some of the brands sold in the U.S.

If these purified options are unavailable or more flavor is desired, other high-proof liquors can be used, such as Bacardi 151 proof rum. There are a number of brands of 100 to 120 proof vodkas and rums that can be used.

Although high-proof alcohols are the most efficient solvents, fine tinctures can be made using standard 80 proof (40%) alcohol.

Tincture Details

The effects of tinctures made with different varieties of cannabis differ because of the entourage effects that the terpenes, the odor molecules, create. Plant potency and post-harvest processing both play a part in determining the tincture's potency. Leaves, trim, buds, kief and hash are some of the choices, and all are used.

Some medical tincture makers have adopted cold-processing methods to avoid decarboxylating the cannabinoid acids. Not converting THCa to THC increases dosage levels because the THCa does not activate the high, but many medical qualities remain.

Raw fresh or dried marijuana leaves can be used to make tinctures, although the resulting product may have a chlorophyll flavor. Gently soaking the dried marijuana in water removes some of the chlorophyll, which dissolves in water. Adding a bit of honey to the finished tincture can make it more palatable.

Fresh plant material is not decarboxylated and can be used to make a tincture. Fill a glass container with herb and then add drinking alcohol (ethanol) to the top. Figure roughly 1 ounce (28 g) of fresh (uncured) buds for every 4 ounces (118 ml) of alcohol. Stir or shake vigorously for a minute to remove air bubbles and then cover. Let the mixture steep in a cool, dark space for two weeks or more. Shake the container daily to mix the ingredients and help the alcohol dissolve the terpenes and cannabinoids.

The length of time the mixture steeps results in slightly different tinctures. A longer soak extracts more cannabinoids and essential oils, making the tincture stronger and more concentrated, but it also leaches out more of the plant's other chemicals, such as chlorophyll. To determine what works best for you, split the batch between several jars that are left to steep for differing amounts of time. Then strain the liquid from the plant material using a coffee filter or strainer. The spent cannabis is tossed, leaving the infused alcohol.

If marijuana has been dried and cured as it would be for smoking, some decarboxylation will have already taken place, so THC and CBD will be present without using heat, just not as much.

For the highest potency possible using dried marijuana, carefully heat it first. Spread the leaves, trim or buds on a cookie sheet and put it in the oven at 80° F (27° C) for an hour, or until crisp. If the oven does not go low enough, heat it to the lowest temperature possible and monitor it with a thermometer. Once it reaches the temperature, shut it off. This decarboxylates the THCa and other cannabinoid acids to active forms. Heating at higher temperatures would cause most of the terpenes, the odor molecules, to evaporate and convert THC to the less potent, more sedative CBN.

There is no need to grind the dried, crisp marijuana before adding it to alcohol because the cannabinoids and terpenes are in the trichomes on the leaf surface. Grinding results in more sludge collecting at the bottom.

Straining

To strain the tincture, first use a colander to remove the large particles. Then use a small-mesh nylon or stainless steel sifting screen. Some people prefer cheesecloth. Line a sieve or colander with cheesecloth and place it inside a clean metal or glass bowl. Cheesecloth comes in different grades, based on how tight the weave is, just as printing screens that can be used for sifting kief are graded based on how fine the mesh is. Cheesecloth grades range from the very loosely woven #10 to the extra-fine #90. Unlike the symmetrical mesh of metal and plastic sifting screens, the number of threads per inch in cheesecloth varies horizontally and vertically.

Use a looser grade for straining freshly chopped plant material; it catches the plant material and does not clog. Cheesecloth grades #60 to #90 are best for straining ground and powdered dried herb for tincture making to avoid sludge buildup. Using fine-grade cloth requires patience because it takes a long time for the extract to seep through. Once gravity has done all it can to pull the tincture through, hold the cheesecloth carefully by the corners, lift it from the sieve and squeeze any remaining solution into the bowl.

If kief or powdered dry herb is used to make tincture, even the finest cheesecloth will let some sludge particles through. A second pass through a paper coffee filter or a #1 laboratory filter yields a cleaner, particulate-free product.

No matter the method used, there will be residual cannabinoids remaining in the mash. To remove some of them after straining, squeeze the solution from the cloth. Fill the bowl part way with virgin alcohol and dip the bud-filled bag as if it were a teabag. More cannabinoids will be captured in the alcohol. Warming it gently on a well-ventilated electric stove to about 100˚ F (38˚ C) makes the cannabinoids more soluble. Caution: Alcohol fumes are explosive so this should be done in a well-ventilated space or outdoors.

Add the new cannabinoid solution to the first one. Place the combined solution in a wide-mouth glass jar or pitcher and cover it. Then let it sit in a cool, dark place undisturbed for several days or more. Vegetative material mixed into the liquid will separate, either floating to the top or sinking to the bottom. The alcohol solution is fairly pure. Gently skim the floating material from the top. Then siphon the solution from the top, leaving the sunken particulates undisturbed. The siphoned solution can easily be purified further using fine filters, which allow quick passage.

BOTTLING AND STORAGE

Once the tincture is filtered, use a funnel to fill the storage bottles. Light causes cannabinoids to degrade so tincture bottles, sometimes called "Boston rounds," are either amber, brown or cobalt blue. However, if the tincture is to be stored in the dark, such as in a closet or other unlit space, the glass color is of little importance.

Glass bottles are widely available in sizes from 0.5 ounces (15 ml) to 32 ounces (1 l). The most common sizes for use with droppers are between 0.5 (15 ml) and 4 ounces (113 ml).

Label the tinctures by variety, solute and date. Storing tinctures in a refrigerator slows degradation of cannabinoids. They can be stored for years in a freezer, where they lose potency slowly. Choose stainless steel containers rather than glass ones, which may crack even though the alcohol in the freezer doesn't freeze.

GLYCERIN TINCTURES

Alcohol is the standard for making tinctures and has the advantage of being a great preservative, but for people who cannot tolerate even a drop of alcohol, glycerin tinctures offer an alternative. Some tincture makers use a combination of alcohol and glycerin in their products. Glycerin tinctures are available at many dispensaries, but making them at home is not much more involved than making an alcohol tincture. It takes just a few extra steps.

If using a pure cannabis oil extract, glycerin tincture is made by adding a judicious amount of the oil to a bottle of glycerin. Figure about 30 servings per ounce of trim leaf. Warming it gently (but not too much) and stirring or shaking helps it mix. Pure USP-grade glycerin is inexpensive and available at drug stores everywhere and online.

If making a glycerin tincture from scratch, start with a carefully strained alcohol tincture. Then add the alcohol tincture to a comparable amount of glycerin. The potency of the glycerin tincture can be adjusted by using either more or less glycerin than the volume of alcohol in the tincture. The final step is to evaporate the alcohol from the glycerin.

One easy method is to heat the liquids in a double boiler. Measure out the alcohol tincture. To maintain the same strength, add slightly less glycerin, because some of the tincture volume is the cannabis oil. Using a spoon or spatula, blend them. The larger the surface area of the mixture relative to its depth, the faster the alcohol evaporates, so limit the depth of the mixture to a few inches. The process is complete when the pan no longer emits the telltale smell of alcohol. Glycerin tinctures spoil in a few weeks if left unrefrigerated.

Starting with an alcohol tincture may seem like an unnecessary step, as it is possible to make glycerin tinctures directly, but alcohol is much more efficient at extracting the cannabinoids and other essential oils from cannabis.

Some people may suggest using an oven to evaporate the alcohol from a tincture, either to make a glycerin tincture or to reduce it to oil. Don't do it. The flash point of pure ethyl alcohol vapor is only about 80° F (27° C), and it takes only 3.3% alcohol vapor volume to produce an explosion. Using a double boiler in a well-ventilated area or outdoors is a safe way to evaporate alcohol.

Sponsor Section

Thanks to all the businesses, organizations and individuals that supported this project.

CO2 Blast [Photo by Lizzy Fritz]

THE FUTURE OF BOTANICAL EXTRACTION IS HERE

THE ORIGINAL RESINATOR IS PUTTING THE INDUSTRY ON NOTICE. Trimming with Co2 is like nothing you have ever experienced... ! Trim 1lb per minute! When you load your machine with flower, you can inject liquid Co2 into the chamber and achieve very cold temperatures. This allows the exterior leaves to become just brittle enough to fracture off of the flower and fall through the mesh screen without damaging, bruising or compromising the integrity of the flower.

WHEN TRIMMING WITH CO2 we recommend "ice-cream" temperature. That's between 10°F and 30°F. When prepared properly, we often experience results that exceed our expectations. The better bucked and big leaved your material, the less time necessary to achieve desired results, only adding to increased processing times and production volume. As a trimmer, the OG model has a 1.5 lb capacity while the XL model has a 7 lb capacity.

Untrimmed Bud in

Loading the dried buds

Trimmed Flower out

www.theoriginalresinator.com
1-877-RESINATOR

POST HARVEST SPECIALIST

GREENBROZ

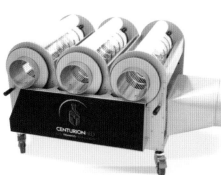

EARTH JUICE

LEGENDARY PRODUCTS. LEGENDARY RESULTS.

Trusted for over 25 years
Providing Quality Nutrient Products for Soil and Hydroponics

Elements™

SeaBlast™

Bloom Master™

BioZeus™

BioRighteous™

Sugar Peak™

GodSilica™

Sweet & Heavy™

OilyCann™

Charts and more details, visit **earthjuice.com**

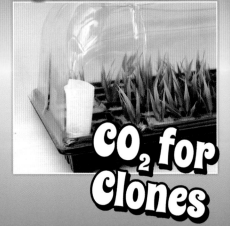

GreenBroz Inc

AUTOMATED HARVESTING SOLUTIONS

There was a time when automating your harvest
meant choosing between speed and quality.
Cultivators were destined to countless
hours of detail work by hand.
They trimmed, de-stemmed, and dry-sifted.

Until one day, GreenBroz imagined new machines.
They were elegant, gentle, well-crafted,
and treated flowers with the same care and respect
as an artisan trimmer. Word quickly spread.
Cultivators began to look at automation
with a newfound respect.
Dreams came true, businesses grew,
and lazy Sunday afternoons were rediscovered.

GreenBroz, the future of harvesting.
Helping you realize your American dream.

GENTLE. QUICK. QUIET.

SCHEDULE YOUR FREE LIVE DEMO TODAY!

INFO@GREENBROZ.COM | 844-DRY-TRIM

LEARN MORE AT GREENBROZ.COM

If you carry smelly things around with you, you need a Skunk bag to carry them in.

SMELL PROOF ODORLESS TECHNOLOGY

The secret of the Skunk Air-Flow System lies in a patented high potency activated carbon technology. Odors & harmful chemicals are trapped and neutralized inside the bag, where they belong.

Skunk
CUZ EVERYTHING ELSE STINKS
www.skunkbags.com

GARDEN NATURALS COLLECTION

Effective, contemporary formulations

Not intended to imply environmental safety either alone or compared to other products.

Look for the <u>tan band</u>

available in stores or online wherever lawn & garden products are sold

You're a Professional. **Trim like one.**

HOW YOU MANAGE YOUR FLOWER MATTERS

WITH BOVEDA

WITHOUT BOVEDA

Boveda
2-WAY HUMIDITY
– CONTROL –

BOVEDAHERBAL.COM | 763.400.3709

TrimBin ™

High walls keep your work contained and make cleanup easy.

150 micron stainless screen produces only fine-grained, high-grade pollen.

Ergonomic design reduces back, shoulder and wrist fatigue.

Easily collect pollen with the static brush and mirror-finish collection tray.

Turn any chair into a comfortable workstation!

Increases productivity by alleviating user fatigue and discomfort.

Made in California.

HarvestMore ®

harvest-more.com

HUMIDITY IS THE ENEMY.
QUEST IS THE VICTOR.

Avoid crop loss. Grow professionally and predictably with the industry's leading line of high-efficiency, large-capacity dehumidifiers. **Find your model and calculate your savings at QuestHydro.com.**

QUEST
DEHUMIDIFIERS

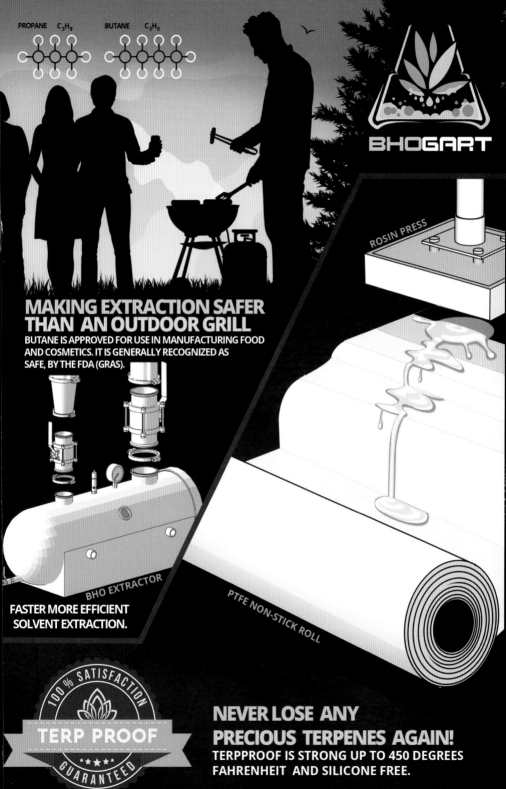

Industrial Strength
HARVEST SOLUTIONS
Biomass, Cure, Store & Transport

100% BPA Free	**Prevent Cross-Contamination**
FDA Approved	**Save Time on Clean-Up**
Contain Odors	**Maximize Shelf Life**
Stabilize Moisture Level	**Preserve Flavor and Freshness**
Vacuum Sealable	**Resistant to Punctures and Tears**

Available in 10, 25, 100 PACK & BULK			
Volume	Name	Dimensions	Tips
Multi-Pack	Flock O' Bags	Varies	2 x Chicken Bags, 2 x Turkey Bags, 2 x Goose Bags & 10 x Quail Bags
3 Quarts	Quail Bag	8" x 16"	Holds ¼ lb, bag tied
2 Gallons	Chicken Bag	12" x 20"	Holds 1 lb, bag vacuum sealed
3 Gallons	Turkey Bag	18" x 20"	Holds 1 lb, bag tied
5 Gallons	Goose Bag	18" x 24"	Lines 5 Gallon Bucket
8 Gallons	8 Gallon Bag	24" x 40"	Holds 5 lbs, bag tied
27-37 Gallons	Bin Liner	48" x 30"	Lines 27-37 Gallon Tote Bins
20-30 Gallons	Ostrich Bag	30" x 48"	Fits 20 Gallon Trash Can or 30 Gallon Drum
55 Gallons	Drum Liner	36" x 48"	Based on Popular Demand Lines a 55 Gallon Drum
---	Bottomless Bags & Dispensers	12" x 100' 18" x 100' 24" x 100' 24" x 500'	Cut & seal to preferred size; Mountable Dispensers cut & store Bottomless Bags

True Liberty® Bags now offers True Liberty® Vacs

20" Gas-Purge, Vacuum and Impulse-Heat Sealer
Adjustable Settings and Industrial Strength Seal
Air Compressor powered Retractable Nozzle and Sealer Arm
Easy-clean glass vacuum filter system
Purge using gas of your choice
Rust-Treated, Powder-Coated Steel Chassis

SIZE
MATTERS

Advanced
Nutrients

Raising the Bud Weights...
and Reputations...
of Top Growers

INDEX

A

Aeon Clean Light, 70
air filtration, 34, 35, 106, 123, 148
alcohol tinctures, 208–9, 210, 211, 212–13
allergic reactions, 120, 121
anvil pruners, 91
aroma
containers that trap odors, 190–93
and dry vs. wet trimming, 129
of moldy marijuana, 148, 169
quality as judged by, 2
and ripening of buds, 7, 10, 78–79
and terpenes, 5, 7, 145
Australia, 105

B

"bananas" (male flowers), 36–37
BHO (butane hash oil), 193, 205–8
Black Out Light Deprivation (BOLD) Tarp, 18
Bolder Cannabis, 24, 107, 120, 190
Bonsai Hero trimmer, 126
Boveda moisture packs, 180
branches and stems, recycling of, 198
bucking machines, 127
budder, 205
buds
burying, 181
flushed vs. unflushed, 31
freezing, 185–86, 193
freshness factors, 2
growing patterns of, 109
mold on, 31, 33, 61, 69, 116, 145, 168
overripe, 36–37, 79, 88
picking individual buds, 27–28, 87
popcorn (larf), 118, 130, 133, 195, 198
and power cutting tools, 93–99, 102
rehydrating overdried buds, 156, 180
ripening patterns and times, 5–6, 10, 87
ripening stages, illustrated, 76–79
sativas' large bud size, 18
single-bud plants, 31
sweeteners, 75
and trimming's purpose, 109
butane extraction, 31, 193, 205–8
bypass pruners, 91

C

calyxes, 8
cannabinoids
botanical function of, 12
light's degrading of, 122, 169, 188, 212
in overripe buds, 36, 79, 88
and tinctures, 208–13
and trichome anatomy, 7, 198
in trim material, 109, 195–98
and water curing, 174–75
and water deprivation, 87
See also potency; THC
cannabis anatomy, 6–7, 30, 36, 39–40, 109
cannabis life cycle, 6, 63
CBD (cannabidiol), 12, 36, 185, 207, 210
CBL (cannabicyclol), 10
CBN (cannabinol), 10, 12, 77, 79, 146, 185, 207–8, 210
cleaning practices
crop cleaning, 106, 173, 176, 205
in curing stage, 173, 176
in drying stage, 145, 148, 150
and microbial contaminants, 35, 129
in picking stage, 81, 89, 106–7
in trimming stage, 118, 119, 122–23, 129
CO_2 extraction, 31, 193
colas
defined, 109
drying or curing of, 147, 167, 176
and harvesting stages, 1, 2
on large monster plants, 26
leaving fan leaves on, 82
and power cutting tools, 96
ripening patterns, 10
and trimming process, 109, 115, 122, 135
and under-watering, 118
commercial and large-scale gardens
clean conditions in, 35, 106–7, 111
drying operations, illustrated, 3, 83, 112, 147, 160–65
picking approach in, 82–83, 88–89
profiles of particular growers, 14–15, 60–61, 142–43, 160–61
trimming approach in, 111, 136–39
and weather-related threats, 68–69
concentrates (extracts)
BHO, 193, 205–8
contaminants in, 31, 35, 193, 204–5
and curing, 183
kief, 114, 115, 158–59, 199–202, 209, 211
sugary wax, illustrated, 192
supermelts, illustrated, 13
tinctures, 208–13
trim material used for, 12, 82, 109, 140, 195–98, 209, 212
water hash, 201, 204–5
conveyor belts, 89, 105
C.R.A.F.T. Cannabis, x, 11
curing, 167–83

in jars or sealed containers, 169, 177–79, 181
in paper bags, 166, 177
purpose of, 167
rehydrating overdried buds, 180
room curing, 167, 169–71, 182–83
skipping this stage, 171, 183
water curing, 172–76
cutting tools, manual, 91–92, 125
cutting tools, power, 93–102, 126–27
CVault containers, 189

D

decarboxylation, 207–8, 210
dehumidifiers, 68, 143, 146, 150, 156, 171, 183
desiccants, 186, 190
drones, 66
drying, 145–65
commercial operations, illustrated, 3, 83, 112, 147, 160–65
judging doneness, 150
"low and slow" approach, 145–46
measuring moisture content, 157–59
and mold prevention, 33, 68, 69, 143
outdoors, 150–55
in ovens, 151, 157, 210
in paper bags, 143, 146, 161, 166
quick-dry methods, 151
on racks, 61, 112, 146
rehydrating overdried buds, 156
steps involved in, 148–49
dust control, 106, 122–23
Dynasty Genetics, 42, 74, 78

E

Earth Juice products, 40, 41, 43, 47, 72, 73
edibles
BHO used in, 207
chlorophyll taste in, 176, 198, 210
commercial products, illustrated, 13
fan and trim leaves used for, 12, 82, 196, 198
and fungicides, 70
kief used in, 199, 201
Empress Extracts, 160–61
ergonomic workstations, 123–24
extracts. See concentrates
EZ Trim Wander Trimmer, 127, 130

F

fan leaves (sun leaves)
judging quality of, 197–98
removing before harvest, 1, 61,

81, 110, 143
removing for light, 30, 110
trimming of, illustrated, 86,
112, 114, 117, 147
uses for, 82, 109, 198
yellowing of, 52–53
fertilizers. See finishing;
flushing
"finger hash," 90, 113, 118
finishing (application of nutrients, etc.), 39–47
bloom enhancers, 72–73, 75
bud sweeteners, 75
chart of finishing products,
41, 43
Ganja Ma's approach to, 143
glossary of common ingredients, 44–47
and plant anatomy, 39–40
and ripening time, 67
See also flushing
Fiskars pruning snips, 125
flavor. See taste
flowering stage
bloom enhancers, 72–73, 75
cannabinoids' concentration
during, 12
dark period required for, 6, 19,
63, 64, 66, 75
and flushing, 49–50, 52, 55–56
light-cycle manipulation of, 19,
64–66, 71, 75
nutrient applications during,
52, 56, 67, 73
stages of, illustrated, 76–77
flushing, 49–61
commercial flushes, 58–59
common approaches to, 52
controversy over efficacy of,
49–50
goal of, 50, 55
nutrient deficiencies, signs of,
52–53, 54–55, 56
over-fertilization, signs of,
31, 53
passive vs. active, 53, 55
SPARC's approach to, 61
time before ripening, 81
time recommendations by
media, 57
and water curing, 173
water pH and temperature,
50–51, 53
Forever Flowering greenhouses, 20–21
freezing, 185–86, 193, 198
freshness factors, 2
fungi. See mold; mycorrhizae
fungicides, 12, 47, 69–70

G
Ganja Ma Garden, 38, 142–43,
182
garden profiles, 14–15, 60–61,
142–43, 160–61
gas-sealed containers, 186, 193
Gaudino, Reginald, 34–36
glands. See trichomes

glass containers, 179, 186,
187–88, 212
gloves, 89, 90, 114, 118, 143
glycerin tinctures, 212–13
GreenBroz trimming machines,
127, 128, 132
greenhouses, 20–21, 35, 69, 111
Green Man Cannabis, 25, 83,
164

H
hairnets, 35, 121, 123, 124
Harborside Health Center, 187,
202, 207, 208
harvesting stages, listed, 2
harvesting strategies, 17–37
30/70 rule, 12
cutting whole plant vs. branches vs. buds, 26–28
and greenhouses, 20–21
and labor considerations, 17
and light deprivation, 18–20
and mold or other contaminants, 31–36
and overripe flowers, 36–37
and pruning, 28–31
and restrictions on growing,
25–26
and supports, 22–25
and varietal differences in
ripening, 18–19
and weather, 22
Harvest More, 119
hash (hashish)
and curing, 183
Empress Extracts' offerings, 160
"finger hash," 90, 113, 118
kief pressed into, 114, 115, 199
and machine trimmers, 133
water hash, 201, 204–5
hedge trimmers and clippers,
93–102
hiring workers, 122
HM Digital, 51
HPS (high pressure sodium)
lamps, 7, 64, 121
humidity
in containers, 177–78, 186–87,
188
in curing stage, 167, 171,
176–80
dehumidifiers, 68, 143, 146,
150, 156, 171, 183
in drying stage, 61, 146, 148–49,
150–51, 156
and mold prevention, 33, 35,
69, 186
at picking time, 88
and pruning, 28
and "sea of green" canopy, 26
in trimming stage, 122
hydrogen peroxide
to clean crops, 106, 173, 176,
205
to clean equipment, work surfaces, etc., 89, 118, 148, 150
water curing with solution of,
175, 176

hydroponic gardens, 40, 43,
56, 57, 58

I
India, 103, 152–53
indicas, 63, 66, 71
indoor gardens
air filtration in, 34, 35, 106
flowering and ripening times
in, 6, 67, 75
frequency of harvesting in,
5, 67
light-cycle manipulation in, 6,
64, 66, 69, 75
picking conditions in, 82, 88
plant spacing in, 26
supports in, 22
trimming approach in, 111,
122, 128
and UVB lamps, 12
iron deficiency, 56

J
jar drying or curing, 148, 169,
177–79, 181
juicing, 82, 198

K
Keirton trimming machines,
3, 131, 137
kief, 114, 115, 158–59,
199–202, 209, 211
Kind Scope, 9
kushes, 4, 14, 63, 74

L
labor
and curing approach, 171
estimating harvest needs, 17
hiring workers, 122
and picking approach, 27,
87, 89
safety and comfort of workers,
120–24
and trimming approach, 111,
113, 115, 122, 128, 130, 135,
139
large-scale gardens. See
commercial and large-scale
gardens
legal restrictions or requirements, 15, 25–26, 31, 35–36,
129
light
cannabinoids degrading in,
122, 169, 188, 212
containers' transparency, 186,
187–88, 212
in curing stage, 169
in drying stage, 149
and fan leaf removal, 30, 110
fungal prevention with UVC
lights, 70, 106, 148
at picking time, 82, 88
red spectrum, 7, 63, 64, 65
for trimming work, 114, 120,
121, 124
UV light's effect on plants'

potency, 12, 64, 110, 186
light cycle (photoperiod)
darkness-interruption methods
(night lighting), 65–66
dark period required for flowering, 6, 19, 63, 64, 66, 75
deprivation methods, 18–20, 71
deprivation of light before harvest, 61, 69, 82
and ripening patterns, 6, 10, 67,
84, 87
loppers, 92
lubrication of equipment, 138,
140

M

Magic Trimmer, 126, 130
magnification tools, 9, 10, 89, 198
medical cannabis
and juicing, 198
and microbial contaminants,
34–36, 176, 177
profiles of particular businesses,
14–15, 60–61, 142–43, 160–61
and tinctures, 208–9, 210, 212
Method Seven lenses, 7
Miron glass containers, 179, 188
moisture content, 2, 110, 136,
156–59, 180. See also curing;
drying
moisture packs, 180
mold
cleaning crops to remove, 106,
173, 176, 205
in closed containers, 148, 169,
186, 189
in concentrates, 31, 35, 193, 204–5
environmental conditions conducive to, 33, 145
and freshness of buds, 2, 61
health risks posed by, 33–35
lab testing for, 31, 34–36, 129
organic fungicides to prevent,
69–70
and trimming process, 116
types of, illustrated, 31–32, 168
UVC lights to prevent, 70, 106,
148
weather-induced, before harvest,
22, 68–69, 143
Morocco, 154
mycorrhizae, 39, 40, 46, 56, 58,
59, 71–72
Mylar bags, 190, 193
MyPharmJar glass containers,
179, 188

N

netting, 22–24, 112
nitrogen deficiency, 52–53, 54–55,
56
North Bay Cultivators, 184
North Coast Cultivators, 14–15
nutrients. See finishing; flushing

O

odor. See aroma
outdoor gardens

cleaning crops in, 106
drying approach in, 150–55
flowering and ripening times in,
6, 10, 68, 75, 76
flushing in, 31
light-cycle manipulation in, 6, 19,
64, 66, 75
picking approach in, 84, 87, 88–89
picking conditions in, 22, 68–69,
82, 88
supports in, 22
trimming approach in, 111, 122,
128, 135

P

pesticides, 35–36
pH, 50–51, 53, 57, 70
phytochromes, 63
picking, 81–107
cleaning crops, 106–7
cutting tools, manual, 91–92
cutting tools, power, 93–102
cutting whole plant vs. branches
vs. buds, 26–28, 82–87
equipment (non-cutting) used
for, 89–90
indoor and outdoor considerations, 88–89
at peak potency, 6, 12, 81, 82,
87, 88
steps involved in, 81–82
transportation of harvested crop,
103–5
plant anatomy, 6–7, 30, 36, 39–40,
109
plant life cycle, 6, 63
plant size, 26–28, 31, 84
plant spacing, 14, 25–26, 88
plastic containers, 148, 186,
190–91, 203
pollen sifters, 201
popcorn buds (larf), 118, 130,
133, 195, 198
potency
and curing, 167, 173–75, 181
and harvest timing, 6, 12, 81, 82,
87, 88
and machine trimmers, 141
and storage time, 185–86, 212
of tinctures, 209–10, 212
of trim material, 109, 198
UV light's effect on, in live plants,
12, 64, 110, 186
of water hash, 204
pruning
cutting tools, manual, 91–92, 125
cutting tools, power, 93–102,
126–27
techniques, 28–31
vs. trimming, 109

Q

Quest Dual 225 dehumidifier, 156

R

ratchet pruners, 92
refrigeration, 1, 89, 185–86, 193,
212

repetitive stress injuries, 121,
126
ripening, 63–79
bloom enhancers, 72–73, 75
and environmental conditions,
67–71
and flushing, 52, 53, 55, 56, 81
light-cycle manipulation of, 19,
64–66, 71, 75
overripe flowers, 36–37, 79, 88
patterns of, 5–6, 10, 67, 84, 87
stages of, illustrated, 76–79
trichome development as sign
of, 6–10, 12, 36, 76–79, 88
varietal differences in, 6, 18–19,
63, 67, 71
Roots Organics Buddha Bloom, 72

S

safety issues, 33–35, 120–21,
205–6, 211, 213
sativas, 18, 63, 114, 131
saws, 92, 95, 99
scissors, garden, 125
Scissor Scrubber, 119
screens, 118, 149, 199, 201, 211
"sea of green" method, 22, 26,
82, 88, 102
seeds
and cannabinoids' botanical
function, 12
and cannabis life cycle, 6, 63
false seedpods, 8, 77
oven heating's effect on, 151
and overripe flowers, 36
shatter, 193, 205
Shearline trimmers, 139
Skunk bags, 192
small-scale gardens
curing approach in, 176–79
drying approach in, 146
flexibility of harvesting in, 5
picking approach in, 87
and single-bud plants, 31
smell. See aroma
soil amendments. See finishing
solvents, 90, 193, 204, 205–6, 209
Soul Synthetics, 43
SPARC, 16, 24, 60–61, 104
stainless steel containers, 189,
212
Steep Hill Labs, 34–36, 175
stems and branches, recycling
of, 198
stigmas, 36, 76–77
storing, 185–93
in cool rooms, 89, 135
in glass containers, 179, 186,
187–88, 212
in plastic containers, 148, 186,
190–91, 203
in refrigerator or freezer, 185–86,
193, 212
in stainless steel containers,
189, 212
and THC loss over time, 185–86
of wet (undried) marijuana,
1, 193

straining, 211
strains (varieties)
commercial growers' selection of, 14, 60–61, 143, 160
differences in flowering or ripening time, 6, 18–19, 63, 66, 67, 71
differences in mold susceptibility, 69
indicas, 63, 66, 71
kushes, 4, 14, 63, 74
Salmon River OG, 42
sativas, 18, 63, 114, 131
and terpenes' properties, 145
sugar leaves, 74, 118, 130, 143, 196, 198
super-cropping, 28
supports (stakes, ties, etc.), 14–15, 22–25
Switzerland, 103, 155

T
taste
and bud sweeteners, 75
of chlorophyll in edibles, 176, 198
and curing, 167, 173, 176
and drying approach, 146, 151
of kief, 199
mold's effect on, 148
and terpene preservation, 5, 145
and trimming approach, 129
of unflushed buds, 31
temperature
in containers, 179, 188
cool rooms, 89, 135
in curing stage, 167, 173, 176
and decarboxylation, 207, 210
in drying stage, 61, 145–46, 148, 151
of flush water, 50–51, 53
and mold prevention, 33, 69
at picking time, 88
refrigerator or freezer storage, 185–86, 193, 212
and ripening times, 67
and terpene preservation, 2, 88, 122, 145, 151, 186, 210
trichomes' brittleness in cold, 186, 193, 201, 204
in trimming stage, 122, 141
terpenes
and aroma, 5, 7, 145
botanical function of, 12
and curing, 169
defined, 2
in kief, 199
and light deprivation, 69
light's degrading of, 169, 186, 188
mold's effect on, 148, 169
and ripening of buds, 7, 10, 76–77
and temperature control, 2, 88, 122, 145, 151, 186, 210
and tinctures, 208–9, 210, 213
and water deprivation, 87

THC (tetrahydrocannabinol)
botanical function of, 12
and butane extraction, 205, 207
and decarboxylation, 207–8, 210
and drying approach, 146
light-cycle manipulation of, 69, 82
and storage time, 185–86
trichomes' color as sign of degrading, 10, 12, 36, 77, 79, 88
in trim material, 195–98
and water curing, 174–75
and water-hash processing, 201
tinctures, 208–13
Tom's Tumble Trimmer, 134
topicals, 198, 201
transporting equipment, 89, 103–5
T-Rex rosin press, 204
trichomes (glands)
brittleness in cold, 186, 193, 201, 204
and cleaning crops, 106
and curing, 169, 173
on fan leaves, 197–98
flushing's effect on, 49–50
and kief, 114, 115, 199, 201
light's degrading of, 187
and machine trimmers, 128, 129
as ripeness indicator, 6–10, 12, 36, 76–79, 88
and screens, 118, 201
types of, 9
on wet vs. dry vegetation, 82, 115, 129
trim, grades of, 195–98
Trimbag, 114–15
TrimBin, 119
Triminator, 138
trimming, 109–43
bucking machines, 127
defined, 109
of fan and trim leaves, illustrated, 86, 112, 114, 117, 147
Ganja Ma's approach to, 143
hand tools and accessories, 119, 125
hand-trimming tips, 116, 118
machine trimming (in general), 128–31, 140–41
machine trimmers, handheld, 126–27
machine trimmers, medium–large, 136–39
machine trimmers, small, 132–35
tumbler trimmers, 3, 129, 130, 134–35, 138
twister trimmers, 131, 136–37
wet vs. dry approach, 110, 111, 113–15
whole-plant approach, 116–17
worker safety and comfort, 120–24
True Humboldt Farms, 48, 80
True Liberty Bags, 191, 203

tumbler trimmers, 3, 129, 130, 134–35, 138
turkey bags, 161, 190
twister trimmers, 131, 136–37

U
Ultra Trimmer, 133
University of Mississippi study, 185, 186

V
vacuum sealing, 186, 190–91, 193
vape pens, 205, 207
varieties. See strains
vegetative growth stage
and cannabis life cycle, 6, 63
and flushing, 49, 52
and pruning, 29–30
and restrictions on growing, 25
strategies for slowing, 67, 71
and trichome development, 9
Vortex Powerfan, 149

W
Wander Trimmer, 127, 130
water
deprivation before harvest, 87, 118
in garden hoses, as non potable, 121
pH and mineral content, 50–51, 53, 70, 173
testing instruments, 51
See also flushing
water curing, 172–76
water hash, 201, 204–5
wax, 192, 205
weather
best picking conditions, 88
harvesting dilemmas relating to, 22, 68
harvesting in wet conditions, 68–69, 143
and ripening time, 67, 68–69
and supports, 22
Wiss Clips, 125
workers. See labor
WPS SmartFlo conveyor system, 105

Y
yellowing leaves, 52–53, 54–55, 56, 57, 58
yields and finishing products, 39–40, 43, 73
and flushing, 50
on large monster plants, 26, 27
and light intensity, 67
and pruning, 28
in small gardens, 5
and water curing, 173

Z
Zero Tolerance fungicide, 70
zinc deficiency, 56
ZipSnip cordless cutter, 99

Bibliography

BOOKS

Bond, Kelly. *The Clipper's Handbook: Harvesting the Emerald Triangle.* CreateSpace Independent Publishing Platform, 2015.

Breitmaier, Eberhard. *Terpenes: Flavors, Fragances, Pharmaca, Pheromones.* Weinheim, Germany: Wiley-VCH, 2006.

Cervantes, Jorge. *The Cannabis Encyclopedia.* Vancouver: Van Patten Publishing, 2015.

Mathlouthi, M. *Food Packaging and Preservation: Theory and Practice.* Elsevier Applied Science Publishers, 1986.

Pertwee, Roger G. *Handbook of Cannabis: Edited by Roger G. Pertwee.* New York: Oxford University Press, 2014.

Pitt, John I. *Fungi and Food Spoilage.* Springer US, 2014.

Rosenthal, Ed, and David Downs. *Beyond Buds.* Piedmont, CA: Quick American, 2014.

Rosenthal, Ed. *Ed Rosenthal's Marijuana Grower's Handbook.* Oakland, CA: Quick American Publishing, 2010.

Thomas, Brian F., and Mahmoud A. ElSohly. *The Analytical Chemistry of Cannabis: Quality Assessment, Assurance, and Regulation of Medicinal Marijuana and Cannabinoid Preparations.* Amsterdam: Elsevier/RTI International, 2015.

Yang, Chin S., and Patricia A. Heinsohn. *Sampling and Analysis of Indoor Microorganisms.* Hoboken: Wiley Interscience, 2007.

PAPERS

Bertoli, Alessandra, Sabrina Tozzi, Luisa Pistelli, and Luciana G. Angelini. "Fibre Hemp Inflorescences: From Crop-residues to Essential Oil Production." *Industrial Crops and Products* 32, no. 3 (2010): 329-37. doi:10.1016/j.indcrop.2010.05.012.

"Boveda Trichome Study." *Excelsior Analytical Labs,* 2015.

"Cannabis Inflorescence - Standards of Identity, Analysis, and Quality Control." *American Herbal Pharmacopoeia,* 2013.

"Chapter 3 - Meteorological Data." *FAO Corporate Document Repository.* Natural Resources Management and Environment Department.

Clarke, RC. "Cannabis Botany."

Cohen, Matt, and Jeremy Ziskind. "Preventing Artificial Adulterants and Natural Contaminants in Cannabis Production: Best Practices." *BOTEC Analysis Corporation,* 2013.

Croteau, Rodney, and Mark A. Johnson. "Biosynthesis of Terpenoids in Glandular Trichomes." *Biology and Chemistry of Plant Trichomes,* 1984, 133-85. doi:10.1007/978-1-4899-5355-1_7.

Daley, Paul, David Lampach, and Savino Sguerra. "Testing Cannabis for Contaminants." *BOTEC Analysis Corporation*, 2013.

ElSohly, Mahmoud A. "Allard Et Al. v. Her Majesty the Queen in Right of Canada." *Expert Report*, 2014.

ElSohly, Mahmoud A., and Desmond Slade. "Chemical Constituents of Marijuana: The Complex Mixture of Natural Cannabinoids." *Life Sciences* 78, no. 5 (2005): 539-48. doi:10.1016/j.lfs.2005.09.011.

ElSohly, Mahmoud. "CBN and Delta -9-THC Concentration Ratio as an Indicator for the Age of Stored Marijuana Samples." *Bull Narcotics*, 1997.

Fairbairn, J. W., J. A. Liebmann, and M. G. Rowan. "The Stability of Cannabis and Its Preparations on Storage." *Journal of Pharmacy and Pharmacology* 28, no. 1 (1976): 1-7. doi:10.1111/j.2042-7158.1976.tb04014.x.

Hazekamp, Arno. "Cannabis; Extracting the Medicine." 2007.

Hong, TD. "A Model of the Effect of Temperature and Moisture on Pollen Longevity in Air-dry Storage Environments." *Annals of Botany* 83, no. 2 (1999): 167-73. doi:10.1006/anbo.1998.0807.

Iversen, Leslie L. "The Science of Marijuana." *Oxford University Press*, 2007, 52-57. doi:10.1093/acprof:oso/9780195328240.001.0001.

Jaekel, Ulrike. "Microbial Degradation of Chlorophyll." *Microbrial Diversity*, 2010.

Karus, Michael, and I. Bocsa. "The Cultivation of Hemp: Botany, Varieties, Cultivation and Harvesting." *Hemptech*, 1998.

Kelsey, Rick G., Gary W. Reynolds, and Eloy Rodriguez. "The Chemistry of Biologically Active Constituents Secreted and Stored in Plant Glandular Trichomes." *Biology and Chemistry of Plant Trichomes*, 1984, 187-241. doi:10.1007/978-1-4899-5355-1_8.

Lattab, Nadia, Safaa Kalai, Maurice Bensoussan, and Philippe Dantigny. "Effect of Storage Conditions (relative Humidity, Duration, and Temperature) on the Germination Time of Aspergillus Carbonarius and Penicillium Chrysogenum." *International Journal of Food Microbiology* 160, no. 1 (2012): 80-84. doi:10.1016/j.ijfoodmicro.2012.09.020.

Martin, R. "Fungal Abatement in Medical Cannabis." *CW Analytical*, 2013.

Martone, G., and E. Della Casa. "Analysis of the Ageing Processes in Hashish Samples from Different Geographic Origin." *Forensic Science International* 47, no. 2 (1990): 147-55. doi:10.1016/0379-0738(90)90208-g.

Mcdonald, M. B., C. J. Nelson, and Eric E. Roos. "Precepts of Successful Seed Storage." *CSSA Special Publication Physiology of Seed Deterioration*, 1986. doi:10.2135/cssaspecpub11.c1.

McPartland, J. M., R. C. Clarke, and D. P. Watson. "Hemp Diseases and Pests Management and Biological Control." *CABI Publishing, Oxford*, 2000, 93-95. doi:10.1079/9780851994543.0000.

McPartland, J.M. "Microbiological Contaminants of Marijuana." *Journal of the International Hemp Association*, 1994.

McPartland, J.M. "A Review of Cannabis Diseases." *Journal of the International Hemp Association*, 1996.

McPartland, John M., and Ethan B. Russo. "Cannabis and Cannabis Extracts." *Journal of Cannabis Therapeutics* 1, no. 3-4 (2001): 103-32. doi:10.1300/j175v01n03_08.

"Microbiological Testing of Fresh Produce." *United Fresh Produce Association Food Safety & Technology Council*, 2014. http://www.unitedfresh.org/content/uploads/2014/07/FST_MicroWhite-Paper.pdf.

Munjal, Manish, Mahmoud A. Elsohly, and Michael A. Repka. "Polymeric Systems for Amorphous Î 9-Tetrahydrocannabinol Produced by a Hot-melt Method. Part II: Effect of Oxidation Mechnisms and Chemical Interactions on Stability." *Journal of Pharmaceutical Sciences* 95, no. 11 (2006): 2473-485. doi:10.1002/jps.20711.

O'Hare, Michael, Daniel L. Sanchez, and Peter Alstone. "Environmental Risks and Opportunities in Cannabis Cultivation." *BOTEC Analysis Corporation*, 2013.

Owen, S.P. "The Effect of Temperature Changes on the Production of Penicillin by Penicillium Chrysogenum." *Applied Microbiology*, 1955, 375-79.

Potter. "The Propagation, Characterization, and Optimisation of Cannabis Sativa L as a Phytopharmaceutical." *Department of Pharmaceutical Science Research King's College London*, 2009.

Pratiwi, C. "The Effect of Temperature and Relative Humidity for Aspergillus Flavus BIO 2237 Growth and Aflatoxin Production on Soybeans." *International Food Research Journal*, 2014.

Ross, S. A., and M. A. Elsohly. "CBN and D9-THC Concentration Ratio as an Indicator of the Age of Stored Marijuana Samples." UNODC - Bulletin on Narcotics. 1997. https://www.unodc.org/unodc/en/data-and-analysis/bulletin/bulletin_1997-01-01_1_page008.html.

Ross, Samir A., and Mahmoud A. ElSohly. "The Volatile Oil Composition of Fresh and Air-Dried Buds of Cannabis Sativa." *Journal of Natural Products* 59, no. 1 (1996): 49-51. doi:10.1021/np960004a.

Russo, Ethan B. "Taming THC: Potential Cannabis Synergy and Phytocannabinoid-terpenoid Entourage Effects." *British Journal of Pharmacology* 163, no. 7 (2011): 1344-364.

Russo, Ethan B. "History of Cannabis and Its Preparations in Saga, Science, and Sobriquet." *Chemistry & Biodiversity* 4, no. 8 (2007): 1614-648. doi:10.1002/cbdv.200790144.

Sexton, Michelle, and Jeremy Ziskind. "Sampling Cannabis for Analytical Purposes"." *Steep Hill Lab, BOTEC Analysis*.

Shehu, K. "Effect of Environmental Factors on the Growth of Aspergillus Species Associated with Stored Millet Grains in Sokoto." *Nigerian Journal of Basic and Applied Science*, 2011.

Wilkinson, TJ. "Cannabis Growth Medium." *Confidential GW Pharamceutical Ltd*, 2006.

Zattler, F. "On the Effects of Temperature and Atmospheric Humidity on Germination and Fructification of Pseudoperonospora Humuli and on the Occurrence of Infection of the Hop." 1931.

PERIODICALS

High Times.
International Journal of Food Microbiology.
Journal of Agricultural Research 15.
Marijuana Business Magazine.
Marijuana Venture Magazine, February 2016.
World Journal of Agricultural Sciences.

WEBSITES

The American Phytopathological Society. APSnet.org.
DinaFem. DinaFem.org.
Food and Agriculture Organization of the United Nations. FAO.org.
Georgia State University. GSU.edu.
The Good Scents Company Information System. thegoodscentscompany.
    com.
Grasscity. grasscity.com.
International Cannagraphic Magazine. ICMag.com.
The Leaf Online. theleafonline.com.
Marijuana Venture Magazine. MarijuanaVenture.com.
Medical Marijuana. MedicalMarijuana.com.
Online Textbook of Bacteriology. textbookofbacteriology.net.
Penn State University. PSU.edu.
Rollitup - the Marijuana Source. rollitup.org.
University of California Davis. UCDavis.edu.
Utah State University. USU.edu.

INTERVIEWS

Alan, and Alix. CRAFT. Interview by David Downs.
Barry. Ultra Trimmer. Interview by David Downs.
Dillon, Stephen. True Humboldt Farms. Interview by David Downs.
Domico, Andy. Altai Farms. Interview by David Downs.
Ed Rosenthal's Online Community. Interview by David Downs.
Evans, Jay. Twister. Interview by David Downs.
Frommer, Rick. Harborside Health Center. Interview by David Downs.
Groco Rentals. Interview by David Downs.
Hall, Ryan. Shearline. Interview by David Downs.
Handelsman, Ivan. Harvest More. Interview by David Downs.
Hoffman, Joshua. SPARC. Interview by David Downs.
Hook, Chris Van. Clean Green Certified Agricultural Program. Interview by
    David Downs.
Jodrey, Kevin. The Ganjier. Interview by David Downs.
Justis, Aaron. Buds & Roses. Interview by David Downs.
Lampach, David. Steep Hill Labs. Interview by David Downs.
Lastreto, Nikki, and Swami Chaitanya. Swami Select. Interview by David
    Downs.

Martin, Robert. CW Analytical. Interview by David Downs.

Moberg, Jeremy. CannaSol Farms. Interview by David Downs.

Mosman, Dana. The Triminator. Interview by David Downs.

'Neill, Casey. Happy Day Farms. Interview by David Downs.

Nielson, Jonathon. RxGreen. Interview by David Downs.

Nikas, Alex. SpeeDee Trim. Interview by David Downs.

NorStar Genetics. Interview by David Downs.

Northern Emeralds Farms. Interview by David Downs.

Raichart, Cullen. GreenBroz. Interview by David Downs.

Rutherford, Charles "Charly". Boveda. Interview by David Downs.

Swanson, Gary. FreshStor / CVault. Interview by David Downs.

Trinity, Josh. Loompa Farms. Interview by David Downs.

Valdman, Jonathon. Forever Flowering. Interview by David Downs.

Weiss, Adam, and Spencer Uniss. Bolder Cannabis and Extracts. Interview by David Downs.

Wurzer, Josh. SC Labs. Interview by David Downs.

Raspberry Cookies cultivated by C.R.A.F.T. Cannabis [Photo by Gracie Malley]